Magic
Base Blocks

For Unlimited Quilt Designs

PATTY BARNEY

COOKY SCHOCK

That
Patchwork
Place®

DEDICATION

To our families:

To two so close to us but no longer with us: Dolores Martin and Tom Barney, who would be very proud of our endeavors.

Our parents, Jeanne and Earl Graff and Phil Martin, who have always believed in us.

Cooky's husband, Steven, who has had both of us to contend with; his place in heaven is now secured.

And last, but not least, the kids: Bruce, Debbie, Iain, and Brenna Schaefer; Bryan Barney; Michele, Tom, Rachel, and Casey McCormack; and Jared and Amy Schock. You have shown patience, understanding, given encouragement when needed, left us alone when necessary, and learned to live with the constant chaos that this book has generated, but oh, what fun it's been! We can't thank you enough.

ACKNOWLEDGMENTS

Special thanks to the quilters who were willing to explore a whole new technique in quilting and went above and beyond even our own expectations with their original designs: Sandy Andersen, Constance Boulay, Chris Campbell, Diana Cutting, Anne DeRienzo, Karenina Grun-Louie, Ange Hampton-Mirer, Barb Haymond, Carol Knight, Jenny Michael, Carol O'Brien, Shirley Ogisaka, Lilly Thorne, Mona Woo, and Selma Zinker; and to Sandy Klop for her beautiful machine quilting. We also want to extend our thanks to Bette Tippett for putting up with both of us for more than two years on this project. She has been a constant source of gentle prodding, encouragement, and never-ending friendship. A big group hug to all of you. Patty has a special thank-you to Sharyn Craig for encouraging her to take that extra step.

Lastly, to each other, for not falling apart on the same day, for trusting each other's judgment, respecting each others opinions even when they differed, showing patience beyond even our own belief, finishing each other's thoughts when that evil writer's block appeared, helping each other attain and fulfill our dream of getting this book published, but mostly, for being what a true friend really is: a steadfast and true believer in the other's capabilities and qualities.

Credits

Editorial Director . . . . Kerry I. Hoffman
Technical Editor . . . . Ursula Reikes
Managing Editor . . . . Judy Petry
Copy Editor . . . . Liz McGehee
Proofreader . . . . Melissa Riesland
Illustrators . . . . Laurel Strand
Carolyn Kraft
Cover Designer . . . . Kay Green
Text Designer . . . . Shean Bemis
Photographer . . . . Brent Kane

That Patchwork Place®

MISSION STATEMENT

WE ARE DEDICATED TO PROVIDING QUALITY PRODUCTS AND SERVICES THAT INSPIRE CREATIVITY. WE WORK TOGETHER TO ENRICH THE LIVES WE TOUCH. *That Patchwork Place is a financially responsible ESOP company.*

Magic Base Blocks for Unlimited Quilt Designs
© 1996 by Patty Barney and Cooky Schock
That Patchwork Place, Inc., PO Box 118
Bothell, WA 98041-0118 USA

Library of Congress Cataloging-in-Publication Data
Barney, Patty,
Magic base blocks for unlimited quilt designs / Patty Barney and Cooky Schock.
p. cm.
ISBN 1-56477-163-6
1. Patchwork—Patterns. 2. Quilting—Patterns.
I. Schock, Cooky. II. Title.
TT835·B273 1996
746.46'041—dc20   96-22450
CIP

Printed in the United States of America
01 00 99 98 97 96   6 5 4 3 2 1

Table of Contents

Meet the Authors

Even though Patty Barney and Cooky Schock came from diverse career backgrounds (surveying and nursing respectively), quilting united them in an everlasting friendship. They discovered they had mutual goals in developing new quilting techniques and team teaching.

Patty's first completed quilt was made more than thirty years ago, but she didn't take quilting seriously until 1979. Since then, she has become obsessed with quilting and fabric. She teaches quilting classes for several local shops and adult-education programs.

Cooky began quilting in 1975. She has designed patterns for adult and children's clothing, and just recently sold the quilt shop she owned and operated for six years. She has taught needlework and quilting for many years.

In 1992, Patty was new to the San Jose area and was looking for work as a quilt teacher. As fate would have it, she was drawn to Cooky's shop. Little did they know at that first meeting what lay in store for them.

Cooky (left) and Patty

Robert Shields

We almost forgot to acknowledge the help of our silent (not always) partner, Samantha. She constantly rearranged the pages of our manuscript and quilt directions. She personally had to try each new piece of fabric to see which was the most comfortable to lie on. Occasionally, she would disagree with an arrangement on the design wall and take it upon herself to rearrange it. She closely scrutinized each sewing stitch. But her most important and favorite job was to carefully inspect and test every inch of the completed quilts for softness and sleepability.

Introduction

Magic Base Blocks? Sounds intriguing, but what does it mean? "Magic," according to *Webster's New World Dictionary* is "the art of producing baffling effects, i.e., as if by magic." "Base blocks" refer to the basic unit in a technique that was designed to simplify the block construction based on large and small half-square triangle units.

With the Magic Base Blocks technique, the cutting and sewing lines are marked onto a base fabric square. The marked base fabric square is paired with a second fabric square and the two are stitched together. After the bias edges are completely stitched to eliminate any stretching or distortion, the magic of this technique begins. The units from the base blocks are cut apart and pieced into traditional blocks or into original, new designs . . . as if by magic! There are two different Magic Base Blocks. Each one results in a different set of units. Magic Base Block #1 is an original technique. Many of you will recognize Magic Base Block #2. This grid method has been around for many years. When paired with our Magic Base Block #1, it expands design possibilities.

The inspiration for this technique came quite by accident. It started with a "vision" in the shower, then a phone call to verify the possibilities of the technique and, finally—to confirm the validity of the whole idea—applying a math formula that worked. This is a nutshell version of what was to launch us on one of the greatest adventures of our lives, one that has led to discovering how two not-so-unusual people joined forces to share a dream of becoming co-authors, co-teachers, co-owners, and recipients of a very fine friendship. It has certainly taught us a lesson about the true meaning of teamwork.

Teamwork is the fuel that allows common people to attain uncommon results.

—Ralph Waldo Emerson

We hope you will take the time to read through the general directions before attempting to start a quilt. If you don't, you may miss the opportunity to realize just how diverse and interchangeable this new technique can be. Not only have we given you specific directions for sixteen quilts, but we have included a "Dictionary of Blocks and Borders," plus charts, to help you design your own quilts. We have also shared one of our favorite techniques, "Random Acts of Stripping," for constructing your own contrasting fabric to use with Magic Base Blocks.

With the Magic Base Block technique, you are not limited to the quilts for which we have provided directions or the blocks in the "Block Dictionary." We hope you will use our book as a starting point to help expand your design capabilities.

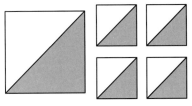

Magic Base
Block #1

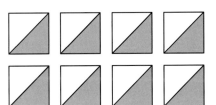

Magic Base
Block #2

General Directions
GATHERING BASIC SEWING SUPPLIES

Quilters love tools, all kinds of tools. But some tools work better than others for certain techniques, so we have come up with the following list of basic tools that work well with Magic Base Blocks. In addition to these supplies, make sure you have *scissors, extra sewing-machine needles*, and *bobbins* handy.

Sewing Machines

For our technique, it is necessary to use a sewing machine. This method is not adaptable to hand piecing. A good straight-stitch machine with even tension is all you need. Remember to always start each quilt with a new needle–don't wait until the needle breaks to replace it!

Rotary Cutter

One of the greatest boons to quiltmaking since the sewing machine is the rotary cutter. This is one of the best timesaving devices available to quilters. The value of the rotary cutter is it can cut quickly and accurately through several layers of fabric. Rotary cutters are available in various sizes and styles.

Cutting Mat

Rotary cutters must be used with a cutting mat. It not only helps keep the blade sharp, but also protects the surface of your favorite dining room table. Mats come in a variety of sizes, some with grid lines. They all have one thing in common: a serious aversion to heat! Take care in storing and transporting your cutting mat. Do not leave the cutting mat in a car on a warm day; it will warp. This is not a reversible condition. Store your mat flat or at least support it in an upright position to prevent buckling.

Marking Tools

There are as many types of marking tools as there are quilters. We have tried most of them, and our favorite is a .5mm mechanical lead pencil with 2H lead. It makes a fine, accurate line, and the lead is always sharp.

Sandpaper Board

A medium-grit sandpaper (#100) surface is useful when drawing on fabric, because it keeps the fabric from shifting while being marked. To make your own board, attach an 8½" x 11" sheet of sandpaper to a firm surface, such as masonite or matte board. Commercially produced sandpaper boards are also available.

Rulers

You can never have too many rulers, but the ones that work best for our technique are the 8" Bias Square®, a 12½" square, and a 6" x 24" or 6" x 12" ruler. These are made of ⅛"-thick acrylic plastic and used with the rotary cutter.

For marking ¼" lines on the Magic Base Blocks, we prefer to use a 2" x 18" lightweight, straight-edge clear plastic ruler divided into ¼" segments. It is approximately ¹⁄₁₆" thick and eliminates the chance of a shadow being cast on the area to be marked, thus ensuring greater accuracy. It should not, however, be used with a rotary cutter.

Pins

Straight pins come in a wide variety of styles. The long, slender silk pins with the small silver heads are excellent for pinning because they do not take such a big bite of fabric. This allows the pieces to lie flat and remain true to shape.

Seam Ripper

We all know what this tool is used for, but it does have other uses. Cooky uses it in place of a stiletto to hold her fabric firmly in place as it goes through the sewing machine, thus saving her fingers from mishaps.

Tip *A quick and easy way to unsew (or rip out) unwanted or misplaced stitches is to use a seam ripper, clipping every fourth stitch on the top side of the seam. Pull the bobbin thread—which comes out quite easily—then place a piece of masking tape along the length of the seam to pick up the remaining bits of thread.*

Masking Tape

Use masking tape to temporarily attach flannel to a wall for a design surface. You can also use the tape as a guide for quilting lines and as an aid for picking up stray threads. We use it to make a guideline for the strip sets in our Random Acts of Stripping technique.

Irons and Ironing Boards

A travel iron works better than a standard-size iron because it has a small surface and a narrow tip. This is especially useful when pressing strip sets. Another great and inexpensive tool is a homemade portable ironing surface. To make one, wrap two or three thicknesses of fleece or lightweight batting around an empty cardboard fabric bolt. These are usually available at your local quilt shop for the asking. Using one of your cotton uglies, wrap the fleece-covered cardboard like a present. Secure the ends with safety pins or, for a more permanent effect, fold and whipstitch the ends down. This makes a wonderful ironing board to take to classes and fits easily in your work space.

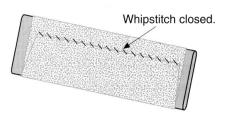

Whipstitch closed.

Reducing Glass, Peephole, Camera, or Binoculars

These are great to have on hand to give you a better view of your design in progress. A reducing glass, which can be purchased at most quilt or art stores, looks like a magnifying glass but reduces instead of enlarges. Using a peephole (security viewer, available at the hardware store) or looking through a camera or the wrong end of binoculars also helps you distance yourself from your work.

Thread

We both use 100%-cotton thread for piecing. Instead of trying to match the color of the thread to the fabric, we found it more important to try to blend the thread color. Therefore, we use one of four colors: white, ecru, gray, or black. This works especially well with scrap quilts.

Design Wall

Everyone needs their own space to work in—including wall space. A design wall is a flat, vertical space that allows you to step away from your work to get the full effect of your design in progress. A vertical surface provides a truer perspective of your work, whereas a horizontal surface, such as a table or the floor, limits your overall view of the design. By using a reducing glass, peephole, camera, or binoculars, you can easily spot any inconsistencies. Other things that may become obvious are secondary patterns you may not have been aware of, an improper balance of colors, or any errors in block construction and orientation. It also helps to view the end product. Does it look like what you originally envisioned?

You can make your own design wall by hanging a piece of white flannel or fleece on the wall. The advantage of using flannel or fleece is that cotton adheres to these surfaces without pins. If you can easily manipulate your blocks or parts of blocks to form new designs, you become more ~uresome and willing to explore.

we first began to develop our technique, ~urselves playing with possibilities on ~all for hours. Every time we turned ~s had found another layout. Refer ~nary" on pages 98–103 to get ~r own design.

CHOOSING FABRIC

Fabric choices and color selection are personal matters, but here's our two-cents worth. Quilters, look in your stash. It will tell you a lot about your personal color preferences. The fabrics in Cooky's stash are predominantly earth tones, and in Patty's are jewel tones. Everyone has their color comfort zone, but this should not prevent you from trying something new. In making quilts for this book, both of us were challenged to work out of our color comfort zones. We learned to appreciate new colors and have now expanded our color palettes.

As teachers, we are often asked, "How can I choose colors for my quilt if I don't have good color sense?" Everyone has good color sense, but not everyone has confidence in their selections. As a learning exercise, go to your favorite quilt store and pick out one multicolored print that catches your eye. Chances are it will contain one or more of your favorite colors. Look around the shop and pick out several bolts of fabric that go with your print. Notice that we said "go with" not "match." For the most interesting quilt, you need to have a variety of textures, scales, colors, and values.

When we speak of texture in quilts, we are referring to visual texture rather than tactile texture. Texture is created by the pattern in your prints. Stripes and plaids have obvious texture, but don't forget dimensional fabrics such as geometrics, tone-on-tones, florals, or novelty prints.

When referring to scale, we are talking about the size of the print. If you made a quilt with all small prints, it might get a little boring. To zing it up, try adding a few larger-scale prints. Don't forget that when you are looking at a large print, you will be cutting it up and only using small portions of it. If the colors are right for your quilt, who cares if it came from a parakeet print? You are going for the overall effect.

There are volumes of books written on color and value. The easiest thing to remember is that color and value are not the same thing. Color is the hue; value is the intensity of the color, for instance, light, medium, or dark. The colors you choose for your quilt will convey a feeling; for example, pastels are reminiscent of spring. Use contrasting values to give your quilt dimension or depth. Avoid using all light or all dark values; the results are often disappointing.

When all is said and done, everything boils down to one fact: you have to be comfortable with your choices of fabrics and colors.

One thing the majority of quilters agree on is the use of 100%-cotton fabric. Being a natural fiber, it is extremely easy to work with and is very forgiving. Always buy good-quality cotton. You are going to spend precious time on your project; you want the end result to be worthy of all your efforts.

PREPARING FABRIC: TO WASH OR NOT TO WASH

Everyone has their own opinion on this subject, and we're no different. One of us prewashes and the other doesn't always. There are advantages and disadvantages to both methods. The obvious advantages to prewashing are to ensure that the fabrics will not bleed or shrink. The disadvantage is that once the fabrics are washed, they have to be ironed. The advantages to not prewashing are that the fabric is easier to handle because of the finish applied by the manufacturing process, and you can start on your project immediately after returning from the quilt store.

There is one standard in fabric preparation that should never be overlooked: always cut off all selvages. Selvage edges have a different density and weave than the body of the fabric and will distort any area where they are used.

CUTTING AND PIECING
Understanding Grain Lines

The lengthwise grain is the strongest grain and does not stretch. It runs parallel to the selvage or the length of fabric. The crosswise grain is perpendicular to the selvages. It has minimal give and runs the width of the fabric. Bias is the diagonal direction of the fabric and has the most amount of give. It is very stretchy and should be handled with care. If not properly used, it can cause distortion in your piecing, resulting in a quilt that will not lie flat.

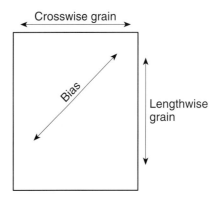

Rotary Cutting

The most important thing to keep in mind about rotary cutters is safety. This tool is extremely sharp, and we've all heard horror stories about them. As a matter of fact, the day after we began writing about rotary safety, Patty had a firsthand (actually, it was a finger) experience. She was not paying attention to what she was doing while using her rotary cutter. Now, six stitches later and hopefully a new fingernail, Patty pays closer attention to where her fingers are in relation to the blade. Use good judgment and don't become another statistic.

1. The easiest way to prepare fabric for rotary cutting is to fold the fabric lengthwise and match the selvages. Sometimes this takes a little maneuvering. Remove all bumps and bulges from the fabric. When the fabric hangs completely straight, cut as 2 layers or fold it lengthwise again (for 4 layers).

2. Lay the fabric on the cutting mat, placing the fabric to the right of your ruler (reverse if left-handed).

3. Line up a folded edge with a horizontal line on the cutting mat. Align the ruler with a vertical line on the mat, the edge of the ruler covering the uneven edge of the fabric. Roll the rotary cutter away from you, along the edge of the ruler, to make your first cut. This is referred to as a "waste cut."

4. To cut the first strip, align the required measurement on the ruler with the cut edge of the fabric and cut along the right-hand edge of the ruler (reverse if left-handed). There is no need to move the main body of fabric each time you make a cut. When it does becomes necessary to move the fabric, carefully align the fabric edges again and make another waste cut. Periodically, check to see that the strips are straight. If not, refold, align the fabric, and begin again.

Here are a couple of helpful hints to ensure safety and accuracy while using a rotary cutter:
- Be sure the blade is closed unless you are cutting. For some reason or another, it attracts children and nosy pets like a magnet.
- When cutting, hold the rotary cutter at a 45° angle to the fabric and push away from you, using even pressure. The blade should be touching and parallel to the edge of the ruler.
- Keep your fingers a safe distance away from the ruler's edge. Blades are strong enough to cut through fingernails, including acrylic nails. Trust us!
- Blades do not have a lifetime warranty. Change the blade when it no longer leaves a clean-cut edge.

Pressing

There is a difference between ironing and pressing. Ironing is what our moms used to do to clothes; pressing is what we do during quilt construction. Hands down, pressing is more fun than ironing. In ironing, you move the iron back and forth to get the wrinkles out. With pressing, you do what the word says: you press. Do not move the iron back and forth; press, lift, then press again. Let the iron do all the work.

As easy as pressing is, you can overpress a fabric, especially if you are using steam. Steam, when not carefully used, can distort fabric. There are only two times when we suggest using steam while making Magic Base Blocks, and we point them out during the block construction.

A firm ironing surface gives better results than a soft one. The result is a sharper edge and a flatter block. This is when the portable ironing board comes in handy (see page 7).

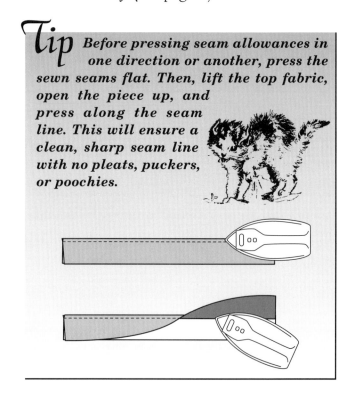

Tip *Before pressing seam allowances in one direction or another, press the sewn seams flat. Then, lift the top fabric, open the piece up, and press along the seam line. This will ensure a clean, sharp seam line with no pleats, puckers, or poochies.*

Accuracy Does Count!

Accuracy is the key to Magic Base Block construction. Think for a moment what would happen if your ¼"-wide seam allowance was off just a little. This ¼" compounds with every seam, resulting in inconsistencies in the finished block size. Squaring up finished blocks to the correct size is not the answer; it only results in corners or points that will never match. To avoid this annoying problem, be accurate in every step of the process. Here are some tips to help ensure accuracy.

- *The cutting edge:* Always measure and cut fabric from the same edge of the same ruler. When cutting multiple pieces the same size, use a strip of masking tape along the measurement on your ruler as an instant visual guide to avoid confusion and errors. If you are cutting on a marked line, be sure you have ample lighting. Your light source should not cast a shadow on the cutting line.

- *Marking tips:* When marking on fabric, angle the pencil point into the edge of the ruler. You can be off as much as ⅛" just by the way you hold your pencil. Keep a sharp point on your marking tool. A wide line also adds to inaccuracy. (What side of the line are you supposed to cut or sew on?)

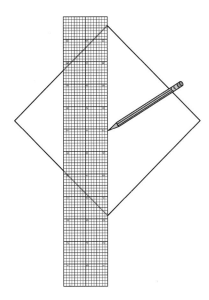

- *Sewing position:* Position yourself directly in front of the presser foot on your sewing machine so you can clearly see the marked sewing line. Sitting to either side of the presser foot is not only uncomfortable but may distort your view of the sewing line.

- *Open-toe presser foot* (sometimes called an appliqué foot): This foot provides a better view of the sewing line. The toes are set wider apart and it has no metal bar across the toes to hamper your view.

- *The infamous ¼"-wide seam allowance:* There are several products on the market to help you achieve this measurement; some work and some don't. Whatever method you use, be sure to occasionally check your sewn seams with a ruler for accuracy. One of the easiest ways to maintain a ¼"-wide seam allowance is with the use of Dr. Scholl's Foot and Shoe Padding. Using a rotary cutter with an old blade, cut the foot padding into pieces approximately ¼" x 1". Place a ruler under the presser foot with the sewing-machine needle directly on top of the ¼" mark. Adjust the ruler so it is straight on the bed of the machine. Carefully lower the presser foot to hold the ruler in place. Remove the protective paper from the foot padding, and place it along the edge of the ruler. On newer machines, which have wider feed dogs, you will have to cut a notch to go around the opening of the feed dogs.

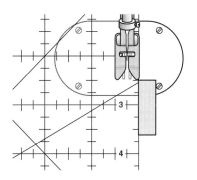

Magic Base Blocks

Up to this point, everything we've written about quilting is common knowledge. But working with Magic Base Blocks is something new. The technique simplifies the construction of blocks based on large and small half-square triangle units. Because pieces are sewn and cut as one unit, problems caused by sewing bias edges together are eliminated.

You will be working with Magic Base Block #1 and sometimes Magic Base Block #2, depending on your block design. See "Diagrams for Magic Base Blocks" on page 91. To order preprinted Magic Base Blocks, see page 91.

CONSTRUCTING MAGIC BASE BLOCK #1 UNITS

Magic Base Block #1 yields one large unit and four small units.

Magic Base
Block #1

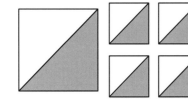

If you are following one of the quilt plans, use the Magic Base Block size given in the directions. If you are creating your own design, determine the size of your finished block, then refer to "Calculating Magic Base Block Sizes" on page 92 for the Magic Base Block size to use.

1. From your background fabric, cut strips the same measurement as the Magic Base Block size. Cut the strips into the required number of background squares. To ensure accuracy, use an 8" Bias Square or a 12½" square ruler as a guide for measuring and cutting. It is very important that all the Magic Base Blocks are square.

2. Using the thin, clear plastic 2" x 18" ruler and a mechanical pencil, draw a diagonal line (A) from corner to corner on the wrong side of a background square as shown. Refer to the Magic Base Block #1 diagram on page 91.

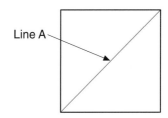

Line A

This is where the sandpaper surface comes in handy. The sandpaper keeps the fabric from slipping or shifting while you are drawing the line, which makes your lines more accurate.

3. Mark another line ¼" from line A on both sides. These will be your sewing lines. Draw the lines dark enough to see, but also as light as possible so they will not show through on the right side of the fabric.

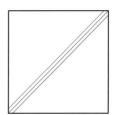

4. To draw line B, place the ruler in the opposite diagonal direction. Draw a line from one corner of the fabric to the intersection of line A. Once again, mark your sewing lines ¼" from line B on both sides.

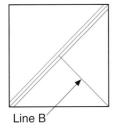 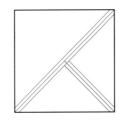

Line B

5. To mark lines C and D, place the 45° line of the Bias Square so the corner of the ruler intersects lines A and B. Draw along the edges of the Bias Square. Be sure the edge of the base fabric is parallel to the lines of the ruler. Your fabric will not fall exactly on a printed line of the ruler. It should fall between two of the ⅛" markings. Lines C and D are cutting lines only.

Intersection of lines A and B

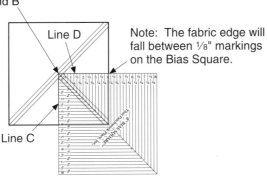

Line D

Note: The fabric edge will fall between ⅛" markings on the Bias Square.

Line C

Mark the required number of Magic Base Block #1 according to the individual quilt directions.

Note: Careful placement of the ruler is necessary to ensure accurate pieces for your block.

6. Cut the contrasting fabrics into the size squares required for the quilt you are making or about ½" to ⅝" larger than your Magic Base Blocks. While developing this technique, we found that it was easier to work with a larger contrasting square and then trim it to size after sewing is completed. When working with the same size squares, it was difficult to keep the two squares aligned.

7. Center a marked Magic Base Block #1 on top of a contrasting square, right sides together. Pin, avoiding any sewing or cutting lines.

8. Sew on the *designated sewing lines*. Do not backstitch. Remove the pins and steam-press the block with the marked Magic Base Block #1 on the bottom. This helps prevent distortion while pressing.

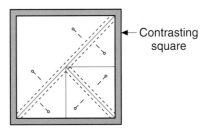
← Contrasting square

9. Trim the outside edges of the contrasting square even with the Magic Base Block, *using a rotary cutter and ruler, not scissors.*

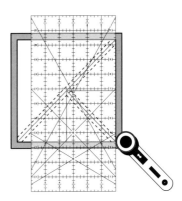

10. Using your rotary cutter, cut on the designated cutting lines (lines A, B, C, and D). This will give you 1 large triangle unit and 4 smaller triangle units.

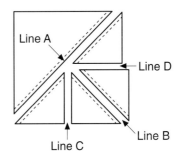

Line A

Line D

Line C

Line B

11. Cut a ⅞" strip from *1 side* of the large triangle unit. Do this before pressing the seams.

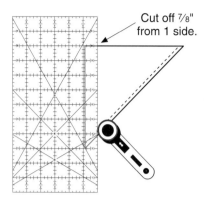

Cut off ⅞" from 1 side.

Note: This ⅞" cut is a consistent measurement, no matter what size block you are making.

12. Press the seams toward the darker fabric. Trim the ears.

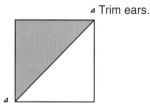

Trim ears.

CONSTRUCTING MAGIC BASE BLOCK #2 UNITS

Some block settings require one large triangle unit and five small triangle units. In this case, it is necessary to make additional small units. Refer to the individual quilt directions for the number of small units needed.

Magic Base Block #2 yields eight small units. The construction is similar to the steps used for Magic Base Block #1, except you draw lines, stitch, and cut the units following the Magic Base Block #2 diagram on page 91. When making additional small units, use the same size Magic Base Block #2 as for Magic Base Block #1.

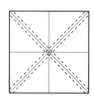

Magic Base Block #2

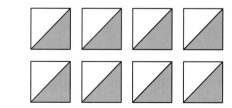

ADDING SQUARES

The block you are making may require one or more small squares in addition to the large and small pieced units. Cut the required number of squares for the quilt you are making. If you are creating your own design, cut the squares the same size as the unfinished size of the small units.

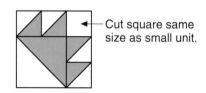

Cut square same size as small unit.

PIECING THE UNITS TO MAKE BLOCKS

After working at the design wall, lay out the units created from the Magic Base Blocks to the left of your sewing machine, with all the units stacked together in their proper positions. The sewing sequence for each block is provided in the individual quilt directions.

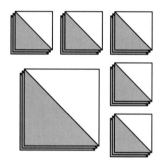

We use chain piecing, also known as flag sewing, to save time and thread. To chain-piece, place two units right sides together and sew as usual. Do not remove them from the machine. Sew the next two units together, keeping them as close as possible to the first two units. Continue until you have sewn all the units from one stack together in pairs. You will have a long chain, or flag, of sewn units.

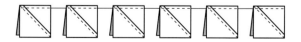

Snip the threads between the units. Finger-press the seams to one side. Place the units back in their proper position in the block to the left of the sewing machine. Continue chain sewing each stack until all the units are sewn together to form the blocks.

 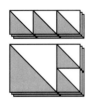

Steam-press the completed block. This is one of the few times we think steam is appropriate in quilt construction.

DESIGNING WITH MAGIC BASE BLOCKS

Many traditional patterns can be formed using our Magic Base Block technique. The most common block style is a Nine Patch, but many Four Patch, five-patch, and seven-patch blocks are adaptable. We have even created some rectangle blocks. Refer to the "Block Dictionary" on page 96 for ideas. Then again, who says you need to follow an established pattern? Why not create one of your own?

To calculate the Magic Base Block size for Four Patch, five-patch, seven-patch, and Nine Patch blocks, see the chart on page 92.

Tip **To achieve accuracy in matching seams and points:**

• *When joining two units that have intersecting seams, finger-press the seam allowances in opposite directions to create opposing seams. The seams will nestle next to each other. When done properly, you can actually feel the seam intersection pop together. Pin on both sides of the seams to secure.*

Opposing seams should nestle.

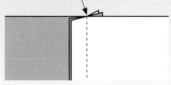

• *When joining two units with points that must match, line up the points, right sides together. From the wrong side of the top unit, place a straight pin through the X formed by the intersecting seams, then*

push the pin through the bottom unit at the ¹/₄" intersection.

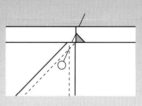

The pin should be perpendicular to the fabric. Pin ¹/₈" from each side of the original pin to keep the units from shifting. The original pin remains perpendicular in the unit. Stitch the two units together, aiming for the X seam. Just before the machine needle reaches the original pin, remove it and stitch just a thread to the right of the X. By not stitching directly into the X, you create a space for the tips to meet when the seams are pressed.

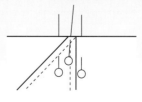

Random Acts of Stripping

Catchy title, isn't it? When the concept for Magic Base Blocks was first born, we made strip sets from leftover strips instead of using a single contrasting fabric. We were trying to find a way to use up all the odd strips that inevitably accumulate. Most quilters (including us) are pack rats and can't throw away any leftover fabric. To use up some of these hard-to-part-with treasures, we decided to focus our attention on whittling down our stash.

The quilt "First Born" (page 75) was our first effort. We combined strips from both of our collections to make the quilt. The fabrics varied greatly in style, color, and width. Even fabrics from the 1960s and 1970s were successfully incorporated. All of our strips were placed on a table and mixed up. This was not a pretty sight. The pile was then divided into two brown paper bags, one for each of us.

Now came the hard part. We pulled out strips and sewed them together—there was no matching fabrics and definitely no peeking or cheating. We had to sew together whatever strips we pulled from the bag. Sometimes the choices were just plain ugly, and we wanted to put the strip back into the bag, but we abided by our rules, kept each other honest, and sewed forth, in other words, in total "random acts of stripping." "First Born" is proof positive that any and all fabrics can work well to create a true scrap quilt.

Strip sets can be substituted for contrasting fabric in any of the quilt directions. For an example of the same pattern made using the two different techniques, see "Off the Wall" (page 78), made with a contrasting fabric, and "Jewels Come in Many Colors" (page 24), made with the Random Acts of Stripping technique.

Follow the directions for creating strip sets to use in place of contrasting fabrics. When using strip sets, you need the total amount of scraps to equal the given amount of contrasting fabric. The key to successful strip sets is variety; the more variety in the strip widths and in the number of strips within a strip set, the better.

1. Cut your fabric into strips, varying in widths from 1" to 2½".
2. Cut the strips in half lengthwise. The resulting strips will vary in lengths from 18" to 22", depending on the original width of the fabric. If you are using fat quarters, cut the strips from the 20" to 21" length to get the longest strips possible.
3. Determine the Magic Base Block size; follow the directions for the quilt you are making or refer to the chart on page 92. Add 1" to that measurement. Mark the measurement with 2 pieces of masking tape on your sewing table in front of your sewing machine. This will be your strip-set guide to help you when sewing the strips together. This is only a guide.
4. Put your strips into a paper bag. Without looking, pull out 1 strip. Now go ahead, pull out the second strip and sew these 2 together using a ¼"-wide seam allowance. Do not begin or end a strip set with a 1"-wide strip, or it will come back to haunt you when you cut your blocks. When sewing the strips together, keep the ends of the strips even at one end. The other end will be uneven because of the varying lengths of the strips. Continue until you have made a strip set as wide as your guide.

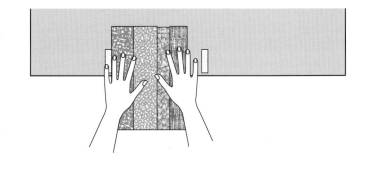

No fair peeking into the bag! Some colors may not look good together now, but when the blocks are completed, this randomness really pays off. Trust us! Even your uglies will take on a new look.

Note: It is okay if your strip set is bigger than your guide, but it should not be smaller because it will not fit the Magic Base Block. Your strip sets may have as many as 10 strips or as few as 4.

5. Press the seams of the strip sets in the same direction. (For pressing tips, refer to the Tip on page 7.)
6. Mark the Magic Base Blocks on the wrong side of the background fabric, following the directions on pages 12–13.
7. Lay 2 Magic Base Blocks on top of 1 strip set, right sides together. Position the Magic Base Blocks on the strip set as shown, so the edges do not touch a seam and the blocks are at least ½" apart. This placement ensures that no large triangle units will be the same. Pin the Magic Base Blocks to the strip sets. Avoid pinning on any sewing or cutting lines. Remember, the more variety, the better!

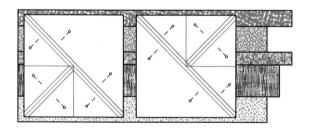

8. Using your rotary cutter, cut the 2 Magic Base Blocks apart. Stitch on the designated sewing lines. Save the leftover portions of the strip sets. They can be used in a variety of ways for the borders or for a pieced back.

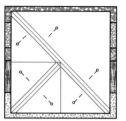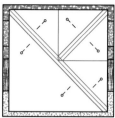

9. Continue constructing the Magic Base Blocks, following the directions on pages 13–14 with one exception: cut the ⅞" strip from the large triangle unit perpendicular to the seams as shown.

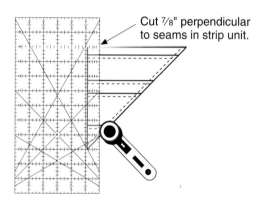

Cut ⅞" perpendicular to seams in strip unit.

10. Press the seam toward the background triangle. The pressing stage is one of the most exciting steps of Random Acts of Stripping. Up until now, you really don't know what the triangle units will look like. It's a pleasant surprise each time you press a unit to see what you get. We told you those uglies would look good!

Gallery of Quilts

If I Had a Garden by Patty Barney, 1995,
Santa Clara, California, 56¼" x 67".

*This quilt was inspired by the border fabric—an unusual design procedure
for Patty; she usually purchases the border fabric last. The backing fabric represents
the reality of her dream garden—dandelions. Directions begin on page 48.*

If It Only Snowed in San Jose by Patty Barney,
1995, Santa Clara, California, 55½" x 66".

*While working on this quilt in the heat of August, Patty's thoughts kept straying
to snowy countrysides, fireplaces, and hot chocolate. This quilt definitely
demanded hand quilting. Directions begin on page 62.*

Arctic Camouflage by Cooky Schock, 1995, San Jose, California, 58" x 72".

This design lent itself to an icy Arctic landscape. The winter animals are camouflaged by their natural coloring. The polar bears are the main focus of the border print. The quilt was made for Cooky's daughter, Amy, who collects polar bears. Machine quilted by Sandy Klop. Directions begin on page 36.

Reflections by Patty Barney, 1995, Santa Clara, California, 43" x 59".

The block design required two closely related fabrics to mimic a reflection.
Machine quilted by Sandy Klop and Patty Barney. Directions begin on page 46.

Cotton Candy by Cooky Schock, 1994, San Jose, California, 44" x 49".

This quilt was created from a fat-quarter packet using our Random Acts of Stripping method. It was made for Cooky's first grandchild, Rachel Anne McCormack. Machine quilted by Sandy Klop. Directions begin on page 38.

Architectural Study by Cooky Schock,
1995, San Jose, California, 37½" x 37½".

The use of two contrasting fabrics creates strong geometric lines.
Machine quilted by Sandy Klop. Directions begin on page 58.

Jewels Come in Many Colors by Patty Barney,
1994, Santa Clara, California, 45" x 45".

*Patty's favorite colors are black, purple, and teal. She actually cut into her
best fabrics to make this quilt. It was constructed using the Random
Acts of Stripping method. Directions begin on page 64.*

Broken Star by Patty Barney,
1995, Santa Clara, California, 63" x 63".

While looking through a quilt magazine, Patty was drawn to a picture of a broken star pattern. She began thinking, "Why can't I do that with the Magic Base Block technique?" This is the result. Directions begin on page 52.

Spinning Hatchets by Patty Barney,
1994, Santa Clara, California, 45" x 45".

*By setting the blocks off-center, Patty formed hatchets. The circular
motion of the hand quilting adds to the spinning illusion.
Directions begin on page 50.*

Oriental "Tee" by Patty Barney,
1995, Santa Clara, California, 45" x 45".

*Metallic printed fabrics give this design, based on the traditional T block,
an Asian flavor by translating the Ts into kimonos. Gold metallic
thread adds to the quilting design, and the border ties it
all together. Directions begin on page 54.*

Serengeti Eyes by Patty Barney,
1995, Santa Clara, California, 45" x 45".

*Patty used various African prints for this quilt. The "eye" was from a
scrap one of her students left behind after a class. It was the
perfect touch for this quilt. The eye motif is repeated in
the machine quilting. Directions begin on page 42.*

What's Black and White and Red All Over? by Cooky Schock,
1995, San Jose, California, 40" x 40".

*The design was originally going to be done just in black and white.
Once the center was pieced, it was evident it needed a little spark.
The red highlight fabric was just perfect. Directions begin on page 44.*

Oh, My Stars by Patty Barney,
1994, Santa Clara, California, 40" x 40".

*This quilt was Patty's challenge to use a fat-quarter packet. All went well until she reached
the border and ran out of fabric. Then her search began for a matching celestial print.
Do you know how many are out there? The results became back art (see page 86).
Directions begin on page 56.*

Canadian Star
by Cooky Schock,
1995, San Jose,
California, 44" x 44".

The design was inspired by a class that Cooky and Patty taught at Stitches 'n' Things in Burnaby, British Columbia, Canada. Machine quilted by Sandy Klop. Directions begin on page 40.

Stitch in Time
by Patty Barney, 1996,
Santa Clara, California,
47¼" x 47¼".

While playing on the wall with Magic Base Block units, Patty discovered she could make a spool design with them. This quilt was also her first attempt at meandering machine quilting. Directions begin on page 60.

Forest Primeval by Cooky Schock,
1995, San Jose, California, 44" x 48".

*The original computer design for this quilt sent Cooky to her collection of greens.
She created a forest that is rich with a variety of green foliage. Change the color
scheme, and the layout could resemble mountains. Directions begin on page 34.*

The Quilt Patterns

Complete directions are provided for making sixteen quilts. Peruse the "Gallery of Quilts," then pick your favorite; or create your own quilt, using one of the blocks in the "Block Dictionary" on pages 98–101. Decide whether you want to make a quilt using two different fabrics or using Random Acts of Stripping, where you make your own contrasting fabric. When using the strip method instead of a single contrasting fabric, the total amount of scraps needs to equal the given amount of contrasting fabric.

In some of the quilts, there will be units left over after constructing the blocks. Use these to make a pieced backing for the quilt, or save them for another project.

Before getting started, here is a list of reminders for using the Magic Base Block technique:

- Be sure your Magic Base Blocks are square.
- Stitch on the designated sewing lines.
- Cut on the designated cutting lines.
- Remember to cut off a ⅞"-wide strip from each large unit.
- Press seams on the Magic Base Block units toward the darker fabric, or if using random strips, press toward the background.
- Follow the piecing diagrams to construct the blocks, pressing seams that join the units in the direction of the arrows.
- Following the quilt plan, assemble the blocks.

The most important thing to remember is to relax, have fun, experiment with your own designs, and enjoy.

Forest Primeval

Finished Quilt Dimensions: 44" x 48"
*24 rectangle blocks, 6" x 8", set 4 across
and 6 down; 2" highlight and 4" border.
Color photo on page 32.*

Materials: 44"-wide fabric

24 assorted beige prints for background, at least 6" x 12"

24 assorted green prints for contrast, at least 7" x 14"

$3/8$ yd. for highlight

$3/4$ yd. for border

$2 7/8$ yds. for backing

$5/8$ yd. for bias binding

For a two-color quilt	
Purchase	Cut
$1 3/8$ yds. for background	48 squares, each $5 7/8$" x $5 7/8$", for Magic Base blocks
$1 5/8$ yds. for contrast	48 squares, each $6 1/2$" x $6 1/2$"

Cutting

Magic Base Block Size: $5 7/8$"

From each of the 24 background fabrics, cut:
2 squares, each $5 7/8$" x $5 7/8$", for Magic Base Block #1 (for a total of 48 squares)

From each of the 24 contrasting fabrics, cut:
2 squares, each $6 1/2$" x $6 1/2$" (for a total of 48 squares)

From the highlight fabric, cut:
4 strips, each $2 1/2$" x 42"

From the border fabric, cut:
5 strips, each $4 1/2$" x 42"

Directions

Refer to "Magic Base Blocks" on pages 12–14.

1. On the wrong side of the $5 7/8$" background squares, mark 48 Magic Base Block #1. Pair the marked background squares with the $6 1/2$" contrasting squares; stitch and cut into units. Pair the same background fabrics with the same contrasting fabrics.

2. Using matching units for each block, sew the units together as shown to make 2 different blocks. Use leftover units to make a creative backing.

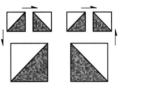

Make 12.

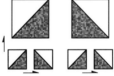

Make 12.

3. Join the blocks into 6 rows of 4 blocks each, following the quilt plan on page 34. Join the rows.

4. Add the highlight and straight-cut border, following the directions on pages 84–85.

5. Layer the quilt top with batting and backing; baste. Quilt and bind. See "Quilting Suggestions" on page 94.

6. Label your quilt.

Arctic Camouflage

Finished Quilt Dimensions: 58" x 72"
*25 rectangle blocks, 7" x 10½", set 5 across
and 5 down; 3½" inner pieced sides and top border,
1½" highlight, and 6½" outer border.
Color photo on page 20.*

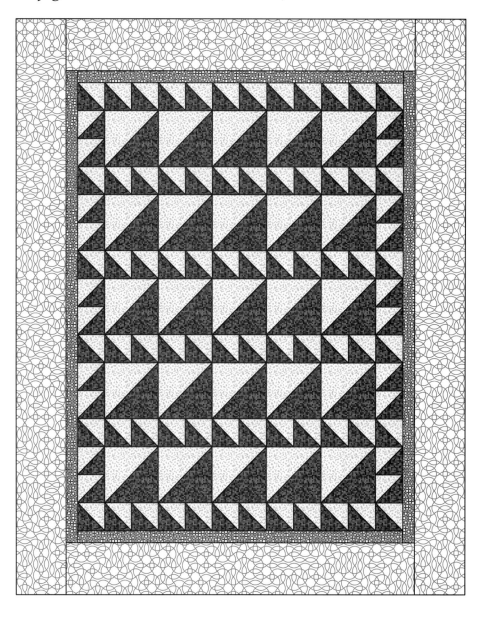

Materials: 44"-wide fabric

2 yds. for background
2⅛ yds. for contrast
½ yd. for highlight
1⅜ yds. for border
3⅝ yds. for backing (pieced crosswise)
¾ yd. for bias binding

Cutting

Magic Base Block Size: 8⅞"

From the background fabric, cut:
   25 squares, each 8⅞" x 8⅞", for Magic Base Block #1
From the contrasting fabric, cut:
   25 squares, each 9½" x 9½"
From the highlight fabric, cut:
   6 strips, each 2" x 42"
From the border fabric, cut:
   6 strips, each 7" x 42"

Directions

Refer to "Magic Base Blocks" on pages 12–14.
1. On the wrong side of the 8⅞" background squares, mark 25 Magic Base Block #1. Pair the marked background squares with the 9½" contrasting squares; stitch and cut into units.
2. Sew the units together as shown.

Make 25.

3. Join the blocks into 5 rows of 5 blocks each, following the quilt plan on page 36. Join the rows.
4. Sew 15 units together as shown to make each of the pieced side borders. Add to the sides of the quilt. Refer to the quilt plan.

5. Sew 12 units together to make the pieced top border. Add to the top of the quilt.

6. Add the highlight and straight-cut border, following the directions on pages 84–85.
7. Layer the quilt top with batting and backing; baste. Quilt and bind. See "Quilting Suggestions" on page 94.
8. Label your quilt.

Cotton Candy

Finished Quilt Dimensions: 44" x 49"
42 blocks, 5", set 6 across and 7 down;
2" highlight and 5" border.
Color photo on page 22.

Materials: 44"-wide fabric

1 yd. for background
8 fat quarters for strip sets
³⁄₈ yd. for highlight
1 yd. for border
3 yds. for backing
⁵⁄₈ yd. for bias binding

For a two-color quilt	
Purchase	**Cut**
1³⁄₈ yds. for contrast	22 squares, each 7½" x 7½"

Cutting

Magic Base Block Size: 6⅞"

From the background fabric, cut:
22 squares, each 6⅞" x 6⅞"
From the fat quarters, follow the directions for "Random Acts of Stripping" on pages 16–17; cut and sew 11 strip sets, approximately 8" x 20"
From the highlight fabric, cut:
4 strips, each 2½" x 42"
From the border fabric, cut:
5 strips, each 5½" x 42"

Directions

Refer to "Magic Base Blocks" on pages 12–14.
1. On the wrong side of the 6⅞" background squares, mark 22 Magic Base Block #1. Sew and cut units, following the directions for "Random Acts of Stripping" on pages 16–17.
2. Sew the small units together as shown to make a Pinwheel block. The large units will be used as is.

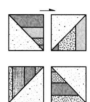

Make 20.

3. Join the blocks into 7 rows of 6 blocks each, following the quilt plan on page 38. Join the rows.
4. Add the highlight and straight-cut border, following the directions on pages 84–85.
5. Layer the quilt top with batting and backing; baste. Quilt and bind. See "Quilting Suggestions" on page 94.
6. Label your quilt.

Canadian Star

Finished Quilt Dimensions: 44" x 44"
*36 blocks, 5", set 6 across and 6 down; 2" inner
border, ½" highlight flap, and 5" outer border.
Color photo on page 31.*

Materials: 44"-wide fabric

⅞ yd. for background
1⅛ yds. for contrast
⅜ yd. for inner border
¼ yd. for highlight
⅞ yd. for outer border
2¾ yds. for backing
⅝ yd. for bias binding

Cutting

Magic Base Block Size: 6⅞"

From the background fabric, cut:
16 squares, each 6⅞" x 6⅞", for Magic Base Block #1
2 squares, each 6⅞" x 6⅞", for Magic Base Block #2

From the contrasting fabric, cut:
18 squares, each 7½" x 7½"

From the inner border fabric, cut:
4 strips, each 2½" x 42"

From the highlight fabric, cut:
4 strips, each 1½" x 42"

From the outer border fabric, cut:
5 strips, each 5½" x 42"

Directions

Refer to "Magic Base Blocks" on pages 12–15.

1. On the wrong side of the 6⅞" background squares, mark 16 Magic Base Block #1 and 2 Magic Base Block #2. Pair the marked background squares with the 7½" contrasting squares; stitch and cut into units.

2. Sew the small units together as shown to make 2 different blocks. The large units will be used as is.

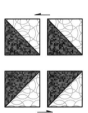

Make 16.

Make 4.

3. Join the blocks into 6 rows of 6 blocks each, following the quilt plan on page 40.
4. Add the inner straight-cut border, following the directions on pages 84–85.
5. Press highlight strips in half lengthwise, wrong sides together. Place on top of the inner border with raw edges even, sides first, then top and bottom. Baste in place. This forms the highlight flap. Narrow strips added for highlights are easier to work with when applied as a flap (cordless piping) rather than stitched as a ½"-wide border.
6. Add the outer border in the same manner as the inner border.
7. Layer the quilt top with batting and backing; baste. Quilt and bind. See "Quilting Suggestions" on page 94.
8. Label your quilt.

Serengeti Eyes

Finished Quilt Dimensions: 45" x 45"
9 blocks, 12", set 3 across and 3 down;
½" highlight and 4" outer border.
Color photo on page 28.

Materials: 44"-wide fabric

⅔ yd. black solid for background
⅞ yd. maroon solid for background
¼ yd. each or fat quarters of 10 prints
    for contrast
¼ yd. for highlight
⅞ yd. for border
3 yds. for backing
⅝ yd. for bias binding (or use bias strips
    from scrap fabrics)

For a two-color quilt

Purchase	Cut
1⅛ yds. for background	20 squares, each 7⅞" x 7⅞", for Magic Base blocks
1⅜ yds. for contrast	20 squares, each 8½" x 8½"

Cutting

Magic Base Block Size: 7⅞"

From the black background fabric, cut:
8 squares, each 7⅞" x 7⅞", for Magic Base
    Block #1
From the maroon background fabric, cut:
12 squares, each 7⅞" x 7⅞", for Magic
    Base Block #1
From *each* of the 10 contrasting fabrics, cut:
2 squares, each 8½" x 8½" (for a total of
    20 squares)
From the highlight fabric, cut:
4 strips, each 1" x 42"
From the border fabric, cut:
5 strips, each 4½" x 42"

Directions

Refer to "Magic Base Blocks" on pages 12–14.
1. On the wrong side of the 7⅞" background
   squares, mark 20 Magic Base Block #1. Pair
   the marked background squares with the 8½"
   contrasting squares; stitch and cut into units.
2. Sew the units together as shown to make 3
   different blocks.

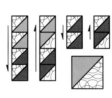

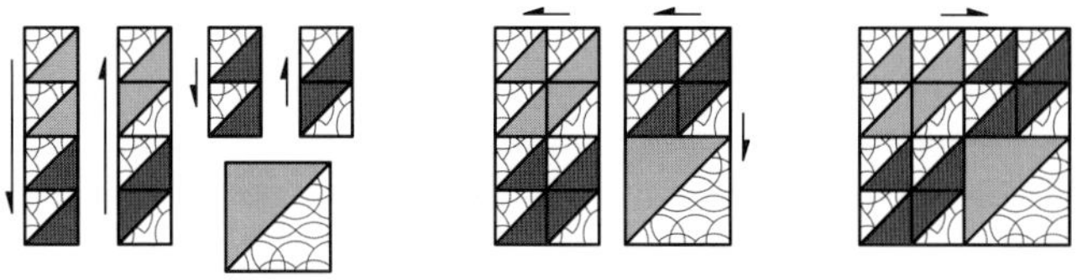

Make 4.

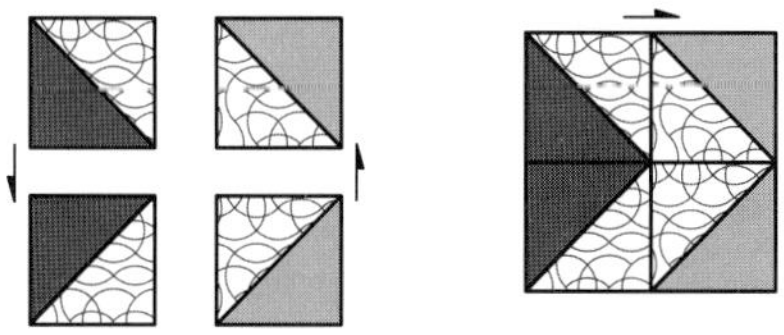

Make 4.

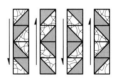

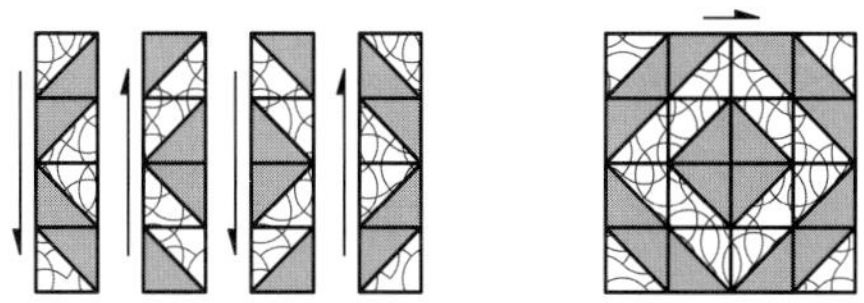

Make 1.

3. Join the blocks into 3 rows of 3 blocks each,
   following the quilt plan on page 42. Join the
   rows.
4. Add the highlight and straight-cut border,
   following the directions on pages 84–85.
5. Layer the quilt top with batting and backing;
   baste. Quilt and bind. See "Quilting Suggestions" on page 95.
6. Label your quilt.

What's Black and White and Red All Over?

Finished Quilt Dimensions: 40" x 40"
49 blocks, 4", set 7 across and 7 down;
2" highlight and 4" border.
Color photo on page 29.

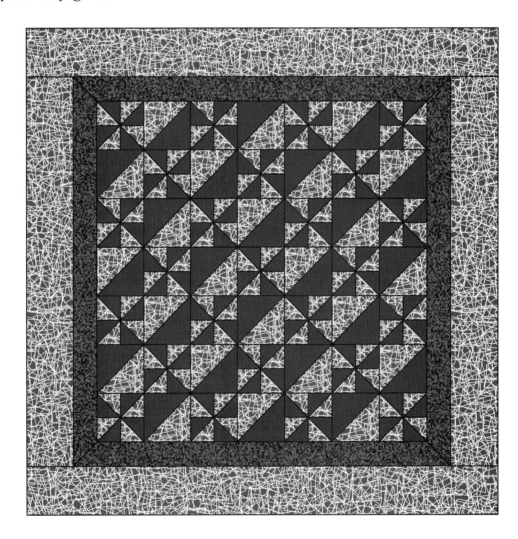

Materials: 44"-wide fabric

⅞ yd. for background
1⅛ yds. for contrast
⅜ yd. for highlight
⅝ yd. for border
1¼ yds. for backing
⅝ yd. for bias binding

Cutting

Magic Base Block Size: 5⅞"

From the background fabric, cut:
25 squares, each 5⅞" x 5⅞", for Magic
   Base Blocks #1 and #2
From the contrasting fabric, cut:
25 squares, each 6½" x 6½"
From the highlight fabric, cut:
4 strips, each 2½" x 42"
From the border fabric, cut:
4 strips, each 4½" x 42"

Directions

Refer to "Magic Base Blocks" on pages 12–15.
1. On the wrong side of the 5⅞" background squares, mark 24 Magic Base Block #1 and 1 Magic Base Block #2. Pair the marked background squares with the 6½" contrasting squares; stitch and cut into units.

2. Sew the small units together as shown to make 2 different Pinwheel blocks. The large units will be used as is.

Make 12.

Make 13.

3. Join the blocks into 7 rows of 7 blocks each, following the quilt plan on page 44. Join the rows.
4. Add the highlight and straight-cut border, following the directions on pages 84–85.
5. Layer the quilt top with batting and backing; baste. Quilt and bind. See "Quilting Suggestions" on page 95.
6. Label your quilt.

Reflections

Finished Quilt Dimensions: 43" x 59"
24 blocks, 8", set 4 across and 6 down;
½" highlight and 5" border.
Color photo on page 21.

Materials: 44"-wide fabric

1⅜ yds. for background
1⅝ yds. for contrast
¼ yd. for highlight
1⅛ yds. for border
2⅞ yds. for backing (pieced crosswise)
⅔ yd. for bias binding

Cutting

Magic Base Block Size: 5⅞"

From the background fabric, cut:
   42 squares, each 5⅞" x 5⅞", for Magic
      Base Blocks #1 and #2
   24 squares, each 2½" x 2½", for corners
From the contrasting fabric, cut:
   42 squares, each 6½" x 6½"
   24 squares, each 2½" x 2½", for corners
From the highlight fabric, cut:
   5 strips, each 1" x 42"
From the border fabric, cut:
   6 strips, each 5½" x 42"

Directions

Refer to "Magic Base Blocks" on pages 12–15.
1. On the wrong side of the 5⅞" background squares, mark 24 Magic Base Block #1 and 18 Magic Base Block #2. Pair the marked background squares with the 6½" contrasting squares; stitch and cut into units.

2. Sew the units and corner squares together as shown.

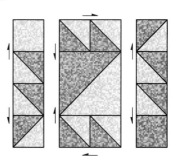

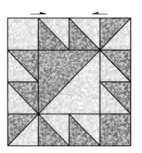

Make 24.

3. Join the blocks into 6 rows of 4 blocks each, following the quilt plan on page 46. Join the rows.
4. Add the highlight and straight-cut border, following the directions on pages 84–85.
5. Layer the quilt top with batting and backing; baste. Quilt and bind. See "Quilting Suggestions" on page 95.
6. Label your quilt.

If I Had a Garden

Finished Quilt Dimensions: 56¼" x 67"
20 blocks, 7½", set diagonally with
alternating blocks, 4 across and 5 down;
1" and ½" highlights and 5½" outer border.
Color photo on page 18.

Materials: 44"-wide fabric

2½ yds. for background
¼ yd. each or fat quarters of 10 prints
   for contrast
⅓ yd. green for highlight
¼ yd. red for highlight
2 yds. directional print or 1½ yds.
   nondirectional print for border
3½ yds. for backing (pieced crosswise)
⅔ yd. for bias binding

For a two-color quilt

Purchase	Cut
1⅛ yds. for contrast	23 squares, each 7½" x 7½"
From the background fabric, cut	23 squares, each 6⅞" x 6⅞", for Magic Base blocks

Cutting directions for alternate blocks and edge triangles remain the same as below.

Cutting

Magic Base Block Size: 6⅞"

From the background fabric, cut:
   20 squares, each 6⅞" x 6⅞", for Magic Base
   Block #1
   10 squares, each 3⅜" x 3⅜"; cut squares
   once diagonally to yield 20 half-square
   triangles
   12 squares, each 8" x 8", for alternating blocks
   4 squares, each 11⅞" x 11⅞"; cut squares
   twice diagonally to yield 16 quarter-square
   triangles for side setting triangles (you will
   use only 14)
   2 squares 6¼" x 6¼"; cut squares once
   diagonally to yield 4 half-square triangles
   for corner triangles
From *each* of the 10 contrasting prints, cut:
   2 squares, each 7½" x 7½" (for a total of
   20 squares)
   1 square, 3⅜" x 3⅜"; cut the square once
   diagonally to yield 2 half-square triangles
   (for a total of 20 triangles)

From the green highlight, cut:
   5 strips, each 1½" x 42"
From the red highlight, cut:
   5 strips, each 1" x 42"
From the directional print border fabric, cut:
   3 strips, each 6" x 42" (crosswise grain)
   4 strips, each 6" x 40" (lengthwise grain)

Directions

Refer to "Magic Base Blocks" on pages 12–15.
1. On the wrong side of the 6⅞" background squares, mark 20 Magic Base Block #1. Pair the marked background squares with the 7½" contrasting squares; stitch and cut into units.

   Note: For two-color quilt option, mark 20 Magic Base Block #1 and 3 Magic Base Block #2. Pair with 23 contrasting squares; stitch and cut into units. Skip step 2 and proceed to step 3.

2. Sew the background triangles to the contrasting triangles.

3. Sew the units together as shown.

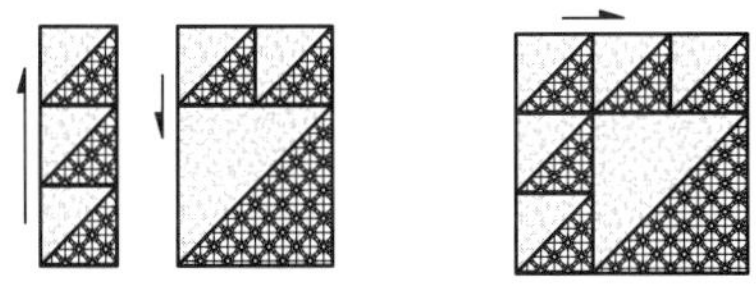

Make 20.

4. Join the blocks with alternating blocks and side and corner triangles into 5 rows of 4 blocks each, following the quilt plan on page 48. See "Diagonal Settings" on page 82. Join the rows.
5. Sew the red highlight to the outer border, then add the green highlight next to the red one and treat the resulting unit as a single strip. Attach the border, mitering the corners. Follow the directions for "Mitered Borders" on page 85.
6. Layer the quilt top with batting and backing; baste. Quilt and bind. See "Quilting Suggestions" on page 95.
7. Label your quilt.

Spinning Hatchets

Finished Quilt Dimensions: 45" x 45"
33 blocks, 6", and 6 partial blocks;
½" highlight and 4" border.
Color photo on page 26.

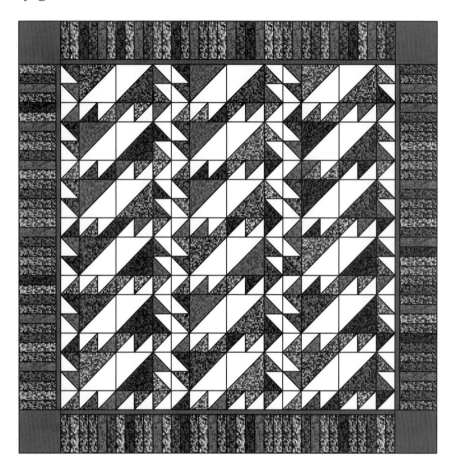

Materials: 44"-wide fabric

1⅜ yds. for background
¼ yd. each or fat quarters of 18 prints for
    strip units and pieced border
⅜ yd. for highlight and corner squares
3 yds. for backing
⅝ yd. for bias binding

For a two-color quilt	
Purchase	**Cut**
1⅛ yds. for background	41 squares, each 5⅞" x 5⅞", for Magic Base blocks
1½ yds. for contrast	41 squares, each 6½" x 6½"
¾ yd. for border	5 strips, each 4½" x 42"

Cutting

Magic Base Block Size: 5⅞"

From the background fabric, cut:
- 36 squares, each 5⅞" x 5⅞", for Magic Base Block #1
- 18 squares, each 2⅞" x 2⅞", cut squares once diagonally to yield 36 half-square triangles

From *each* of the contrasting fabrics, cut:
- 2 squares, each 6½" x 6½" (for a total of 36 squares)
- 1 square, 2⅞" x 2⅞"; cut once diagonally to yield 2 half-square triangles (for a total of 36 triangles)

For pieced border, cut remainder of contrasting fabrics into 144 strips, each 1½" x 4½"

From the highlight fabric, cut:
- 4 strips, each 1" x 36½"
- 4 squares, each 5" x 5", for corners

Directions

Refer to "Magic Base Blocks" on pages 12–14.

1. On the wrong side of the 5⅞" background squares, mark 36 Magic Base Block #1. Pair the marked background squares with the 6½" contrasting squares; stitch and cut into units.

   Note: For two-color quilt option, mark 36 Magic Base Block #1 and 5 Magic Base Block #2. Pair with 41 contrasting squares; stitch and cut into units. Skip step 2 and proceed to step 3.

2. Sew the background triangles to the contrasting triangles.

3. Sew the units together as shown to make 3 different blocks.

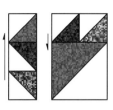 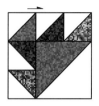

Make 33.

Make 3.

Make 3.

4. Join the blocks into 3 vertical rows of 6 blocks each and 3 vertical rows of 5 blocks and 2 partial blocks as shown. Join the rows.

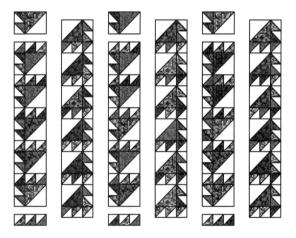

5. Sew 36 contrasting 1½" x 4½" strips together on the long sides to make each of the 4 pieced border strips; they should measure 4½" x 36½". Press all the seams in one direction.

6. Sew a 1" x 36½" highlight strip to one long side of each pieced border strip.

7. Sew 2 pieced borders to the sides of the quilt. Add a corner square to each end of the remaining pieced border strips; sew to the top and bottom edges.

8. Layer the quilt top with batting and backing; baste. Quilt and bind. See "Quilting Suggestions" on page 96.

9. Label your quilt.

Broken Star

Finished Quilt Dimensions: 63" x 63"
100 blocks, 5", set 10 across and 10 down;
1" highlight and 5½" border.
Color photo on page 25.

Materials: 44"-wide fabric

1⅞ yds. for background
1⅔ yds. for contrasting Fabric A
1⅔ yds. for contrasting Fabric B
⅜ yd. for highlight
1½ yds. for border
3⅞ yds. for backing
¾ yd. for bias binding

Cutting

Magic Base Block Size: 6⅞"

From the background fabric, cut:
  32 squares, each 6⅞" x 6⅞", for Magic Base Block #1
  16 squares, each 5½" x 5½"
From Fabric A, cut:
  16 squares, each 6⅞" x 6⅞", for Magic Base Block #1
  16 squares, each 7½" x 7½"
From Fabric B, cut:
  32 squares, each 7½" x 7½"
From the highlight fabric, cut:
  6 strips, each 1½" x 42"
From the border fabric, cut:
  8 strips, each 6" x 42"

Directions

Refer to "Magic Base Blocks" on pages 12–14.
 1. On the wrong side of the 6⅞" background squares, mark 32 Magic Base Block #1; on the wrong side of the 6⅞" Fabric A squares, mark 16 Magic Base Block #1.
 2. Pair the 32 marked background squares with 16 Fabric A 7½" squares and 16 Fabric B 7½" squares. Pair the 16 marked Fabric A squares with 16 Fabric B 7½" squares; stitch and cut into units.

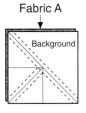
Fabric A
Background
Make 16.

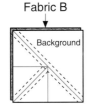
Fabric B
Background
Make 16.

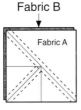
Fabric B
Fabric A
Make 16.

 3. Sew the small units together as shown to make 3 different blocks. The large units will be used as is.

 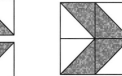

Fabric A
Make 16.

Fabric B
Make 16.

Fabrics A and B
Make 4.

 4. Join the blocks and 5½" background squares into 10 rows of 10 blocks each, following the quilt plan on page 52.
 5. Add the highlight and border, following the directions for "Mitered Borders" on page 85.
 6. Layer the quilt top with batting and backing; baste. Quilt and bind. See "Quilting Suggestions" on page 96.
 7. Label your quilt.

Oriental "Tee"

Finished Quilt Dimensions: 45" x 45"
36 blocks, 6", set 6 across and 6 down;
1" highlight and 3½" border.
Color photo on page 27.

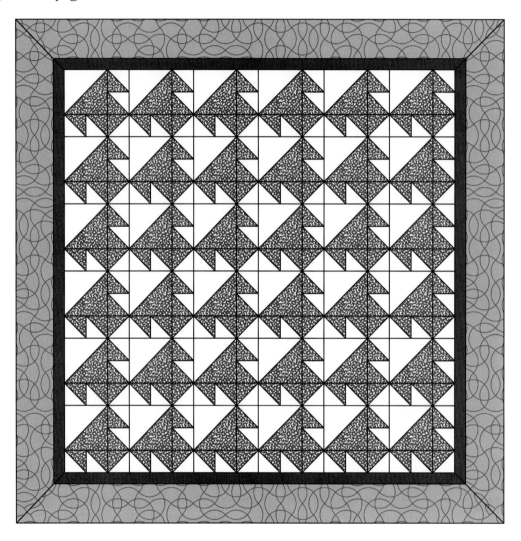

Materials: 44"-wide fabric

1¼ yds. for background
¼ yd. each or fat quarters of 18 prints for contrast
¼ yd. for highlight
1½ yds. directional print for border (strips cut on lengthwise grain)*
3 yds. for backing
⅝ yd. for bias binding

*Or ¾ yd. for border strips cut on the crosswise grain

For a two-color quilt	
Purchase	**Cut**
1⅛ yds. for background	41 squares, each 5⅞" x 5⅞", for Magic Base blocks
1½ yds. for contrast	41 squares, each 6½" x 6½"

Cutting

Magic Base Block Size: 5⅞"

From the background fabric, cut:
36 squares, each 5⅞" x 5⅞", for Magic Base Block #1
18 squares, each 2⅞" x 2⅞"; cut squares once diagonally to yield 36 half-square triangles

From *each* of the 18 contrasting prints, cut:
2 squares, each 6½" x 6½" (for a total of 36 squares)
1 square, 2⅞" x 2⅞"; cut squares once diagonally to yield 2 half-square triangles (for a total of 36 triangles)

From the highlight fabric, cut:
4 strips, each 1½" x 42"

From the border fabric, cut:
4 strips, each 4" x 50" (cut on lengthwise grain of fabric) or 5 strips, each 4" x 42" (cut on crosswise grain)

Directions

Refer to "Magic Base Blocks" on pages 12–15.
1. On the wrong side of the 5⅞" background squares, mark 36 Magic Base Block #1. Pair the marked background squares with the 6½" contrasting squares; stitch and cut into units.

Note: For two-color quilt option, mark 36 Magic Base Block #1 and 5 Magic Base Block #2. Pair with 41 contrasting squares; stitch and cut into units. Skip step 2 and proceed to step 3.

2. Sew the background triangles to the contrasting triangles.

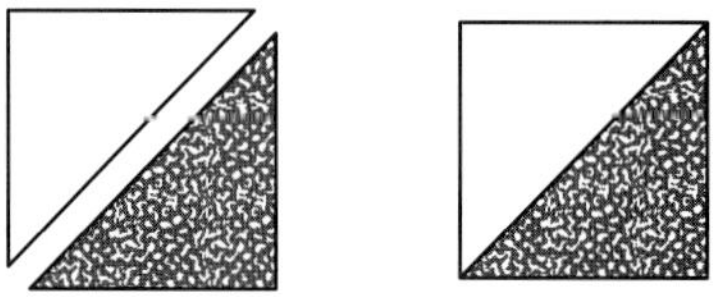

3. Using matching units, sew the units together as shown.

 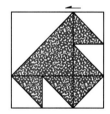

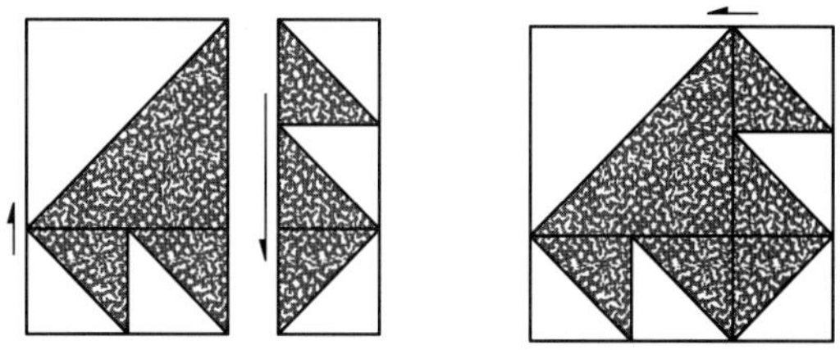

Make 36.

4. Join the blocks into 6 rows of 6 blocks each, following the quilt plan on page 54. Join the rows.
5. Add the highlight and border, following the directions for "Mitered Borders" on page 85.
6. Layer the quilt top with batting and backing; baste. Quilt and bind. See "Quilting Suggestions" on page 96.
7. Label your quilt.

Oh, My Stars

Finished Quilt Dimensions: 40" x 40"

16 blocks, 7½", set 4 across and 4 down;

½" highlight and 4½" borders.

Color photo on page 30.

Materials: 44"-wide fabric

¾ yd. for background
8 fat quarters for strip sets
¼ yd. lamé for strip sets
¼ yd. iron-on interfacing for lamé*
¼ yd. for highlight
⅜ yd. each of 2 different prints for border
1⅓ yds. for backing
⅔ yd. for bias binding

*Press the iron-on interfacing to the back side of the lamé.

For a two-color quilt	
Purchase	**Cut**
1 yd. for contrast	18 squares, each 7½" x 7½"
⅔ yd. for border	4 strips, each 5" x 42"

Cutting

Magic Base Block Size: 6⅞"

From the background fabric, cut:
18 squares, each 6⅞" x 6⅞", for Magic Base Blocks #1 and #2

From the fat quarters and the lamé, follow the directions for "Random Acts of Stripping" on pages 16–17; cut and sew 9 strip sets, approximately 8" x 20".

From the highlight fabric, cut:
4 strips, each 1" x 42"

From *each* of the 2 prints for border, cut:
2 strips, each 5" x 42"

Directions

Refer to "Magic Base Blocks" on pages 12–15.

1. On the wrong side of the 6⅞" background squares, mark 16 Magic Base Block #1 and 2 Magic Base Block #2. Sew and cut units according to the directions in "Random Acts of Stripping" on pages 16–17.

2. Sew the units together as shown.

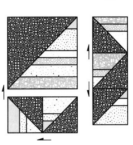 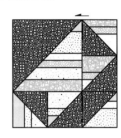

Make 16.

3. Join the blocks into 4 rows of 4 blocks each, following the quilt plan on page 56. Join the rows.

4. Add the highlight and border, following the directions for "Mitered Borders" on page 85.

5. Layer the quilt top with batting and backing; baste. Quilt and bind. See "Quilting Suggestions" on page 96.

6. Label your quilt.

Architectural Study

Finished Quilt Dimensions: 37½" x 37½"

21 rectangular blocks, 5" x 7½";

1¼" highlight and 2½" border.

Color photo on page 23.

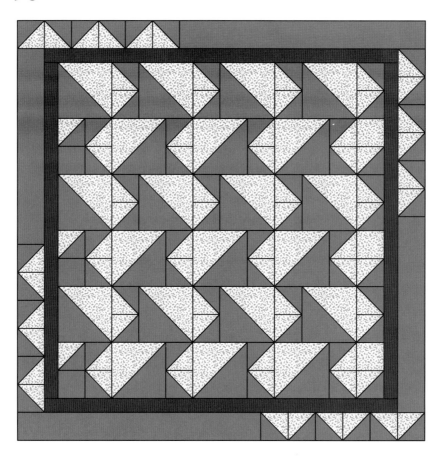

Materials: 44"-wide fabric

1 yd. for background

1¼ yds. for contrast

⅜ yd. for highlight

⅜ yd. for border

1¼ yds. for backing

½ yd. for bias binding

Cutting

Magic Base Block Size: 6⅞"

From the background fabric, cut:

21 squares, each 6⅞" x 6⅞", for Magic Base Block #1

3 squares, each 3" x 3"

From the contrasting fabric, cut:

21 squares, each 7½" x 7½"

3 squares, each 3" x 3"

From the highlight fabric, cut:

4 strips, each 1¾" x 42"

From the border fabric, cut:

2 strips, each 3" x 18"

2 strips, each 3" x 23"

Directions

Refer to "Magic Base Blocks" on pages 12–14.

1. On the wrong side of the 6⅞" background squares, mark 21 Magic Base Block #1. Pair the marked background squares with the 7½" contrasting squares; stitch and cut into units.

2. Sew the units and 3" squares together as shown.

  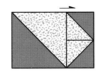

Make 12.

Make 3.

Make 9.

Make 3.

3. Join the blocks into 3 rows of 4 blocks each, and 3 rows of 3 blocks and 2 partial blocks as shown.

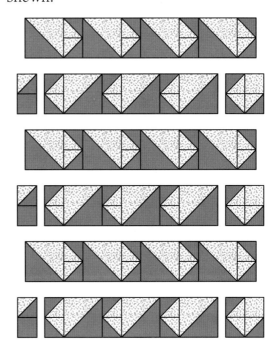

4. Add the highlight, following the directions on pages 84–85.

5. Sew 6 small units together to make each of 4 pieced borders sets. Sew a 3" x 18" border strip to the left end of 2 border sets. Attach these to the sides of the quilt. Sew a 3" x 23" border strip to the left end of the remaining 2 border sets, and add these to the top and bottom edges of the quilt. Make sure the triangle units are oriented as shown in the quilt plan.

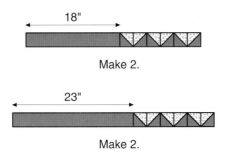

Make 2.

Make 2.

6. Layer the quilt top with batting and backing; baste. Quilt and bind. See "Quilting Suggestions" on page 97.

7. Label your quilt.

Stitch in Time

Finished Quilt Dimensions: 47¼" x 47¼"

7 blocks, 10", set on point;

two 1" highlights and 5" border.

Color photo on page 31.

Materials: 44"-wide fabric

1⅜ yds. for background

¼ yd. each or fat quarters of 7 shades of
    red for contrast (includes pieced border)

½ yd. for highlights

3 yd. for backing

⅔ yd. for bias binding

For a two-color quilt	
Purchase	**Cut**
⅞ yd. for contrast	14 squares, each 7½" x 7½"
1⅛ yds. for border	6 strips, each 5½" x 42"

Cutting

Magic Base Block Size: 6⅞"

From the background fabric, cut:
  14 squares, each 6⅞" x 6⅞", for Magic Base Block #1
  4 rectangles, each 5½" x 10½"
  2 squares, each 13⅝" x 13⅝"; cut squares once diagonally to yield 4 half-square triangles

From each of the 7 reds, cut:
  2 squares, each 7½" x 7½"
  For pieced border, cut enough strips in random widths and 5½" long to construct 8 pieced borders, each 5½" x 27".

From the highlight fabric, cut:
  8 strips, each 1½" x 42"

Directions

Refer to "Magic Base Blocks" on pages 12–14.
1. On the wrong side of the 6⅞" background squares, mark 14 Magic Base Block #1. Pair the marked background squares with the 7½" red squares; stitch and cut into units.
2. Sew the units together as shown.

Make 14.

Make 7.

3. Join the blocks into 1 row of 3 blocks each, and 2 rows of 2 blocks with 2 rectangles each as shown.

4. Add the first highlight border, following the directions on pages 84–85.

5. Sew the second set of highlight strips to the short sides of each large half-square triangle as shown.

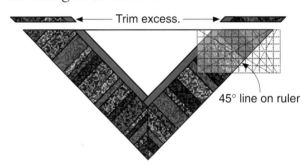

6. Join the random widths of 5½"-long strips together on the long sides to make a border 27" long. Make a total of 8 pieced borders. You may end up cutting some off, but it is better to have too much than not enough.
7. Sew the pieced border strips to the short sides of the large triangles; miter the corners, following the directions for "Mitered Borders" on page 85. Trim the excess pieced border from the triangles as shown.

Trim excess.

45° line on ruler

8. Sew 2 pieced corners to opposite ends of the quilt. Press the seams toward the corners. Sew 2 pieced corners to the remaining sides.

9. Layer the quilt top with batting and backing; baste. Quilt and bind. See "Quilting Suggestions" on page 97.
10. Label your quilt.

If It Only Snowed in San Jose

Finished Quilt Dimensions: 55½" x 66"
20 blocks, 10½", set 4 across and 5 down; two ⅝"
highlights and 5½" border.
Color photo on page 19.

Materials: 44"-wide fabric

1⅞ yds. for background
¼ yd. each or fat quarters of 20
    contrasting plaids and stripes
⅓ yd. green for highlight
⅓ yd. yellow for highlight
1¼ yds. for border
3½ yds. for backing (pieced crosswise)
⅔ yd. for bias binding

For a two-color quilt	
Purchase	**Cut**
2½ yds. for contrast	80 squares, each 5½" x 5½
	80 strips, each 2" x 5"

Cutting

Magic Base Block Size: 4⅞"

From the background fabric, cut:
    80 squares, each 4⅞" x 4⅞", for Magic Base
      Block #1
    100 squares, each 2" x 2", for corners and
      centers
**From *each* of the contrasting plaids and
stripes, cut:**
    4 squares, each 5½" x 5½" (for a total of
      80 squares)
    4 strips, each 2" x 5" (for a total of 80 strips)
From the green highlight, cut:
    6 strips, each 1⅛" x 42"
From the yellow highlight, cut:
    6 strips, each 1⅛" x 42"
From the border fabric, cut:
    6 strips, each 6" x 42"

Directions

Refer to "Magic Base Blocks" on pages 12–14

1. On the wrong side of the 4⅞" background squares, mark 80 Magic Base Block #1. Pair the marked background squares with the 5½" contrasting squares; stitch and cut into units.
2. Lay out the units on your design wall, mixing the plaids and stripes to create a pleasing arrangement. Patty used 3 contrasting plaids and stripes in each block: 1 for the small units, 1 for the large units, and 1 for the cross pieces. Sew the units together as shown.

Make 80.

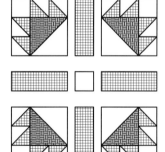 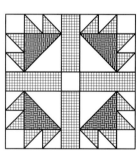

Make 20.

3. Join the blocks in 4 rows of 5 blocks each, following the quilt plan on page 62. Join the rows.
4. Add the 2 highlights and straight-cut border, following the directions on pages 84–85.
5. Layer the quilt top with batting and backing; baste. Quilt and bind. See "Quilting Suggestions" on page 97.
6. Label your quilt.

Jewels Come in Many Colors

Finished Quilt Dimensions: 45" x 45"
16 blocks, 7½", set on point;
two ¾" highlights and a 4½" border.
Color photo on page 24.

Materials: 44"-wide fabric

1⅛ yds. for background
2 yds. total of 8 contrasting fabrics for strip
    sets, highlights, and border
3 yds. for backing
⅔ yd. for bias binding

For a two-color quilt	
Purchase	**Cut**
1 yd. for contrast	18 squares, each 7½" x 7½"
¼ yd. for highlights	5 strips, each 1¼" x 42"
⅞ yd. for border	5 strips, each 5" x 42"

Cutting

Magic Base Block Size: 6⅞"

From the background fabric, cut:
18 squares, each 6⅞" x 6⅞", for 16 Magic Base Block #1 and 2 Magic Base Block #2
2 squares, each 13⅝" x 13⅝"; cut squares once diagonally to yield 4 half-square triangles

From the contrasting fabrics, follow the directions for "Random Acts of Stripping" on pages 16–17; cut and sew 9 strip sets, approximately 8" x 20"

From *each* of 8 different contrasting fabrics, cut:
1 strip, 1¼" x 42" (for a total of 8 strips), for highlights

Directions

Refer to "Magic Base Blocks" on pages 12–15.
1. On the wrong side of the 6⅞" background squares, mark 16 Magic Base Block #1 and 2 Magic Base Block #2. Sew and cut units, following the directions for "Random Acts of Stripping" on pages 16–17.
2. Sew the units together as shown.

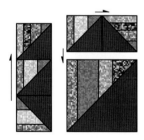 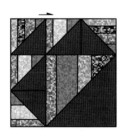

Make 16.

3. Join the blocks into 4 rows of 4 blocks each, following the quilt plan on page 64. Join the rows.
4. Using a different highlight for each side, attach the highlights, following the directions on pages 84–85.
5. Sew a highlight strip to the short sides of each large half-square triangle. Do not miter the corners.

6. Using leftover strip-set fabric, join enough 5" strips together on the long sides to measure approximately 26" for the pieced borders. Make 8 pieced borders. You may end up cutting some off, but it is better to have too much than not enough.
7. Sew the pieced border strips to the short sides of the large triangles; miter the corners, following the directions for "Mitered Borders" on page 85. Trim the excess pieced border from the triangle as shown.

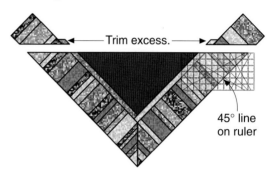

Trim excess.

45° line on ruler

8. Sew 2 pieced corners to opposite sides of the quilt. Press the seams toward the corners. Sew 2 pieced corners to the remaining sides.

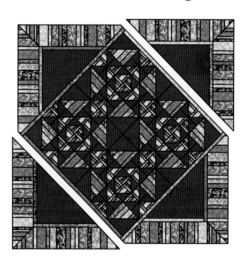

9. Layer the quilt top with batting and backing; baste. Quilt and bind. See "Quilting Suggestions" on page 97.
10. Label your quilt.

Quilts for Inspiration

A Few of My Favorite Things by Jenny Michael,
1995, Saratoga, California, 52" x 52".

*This quilt started as a Sawtooth Star and evolved into a collection of Jenny's
favorite things. This is also one of her husband's favorite quilts. Machine quilted.*

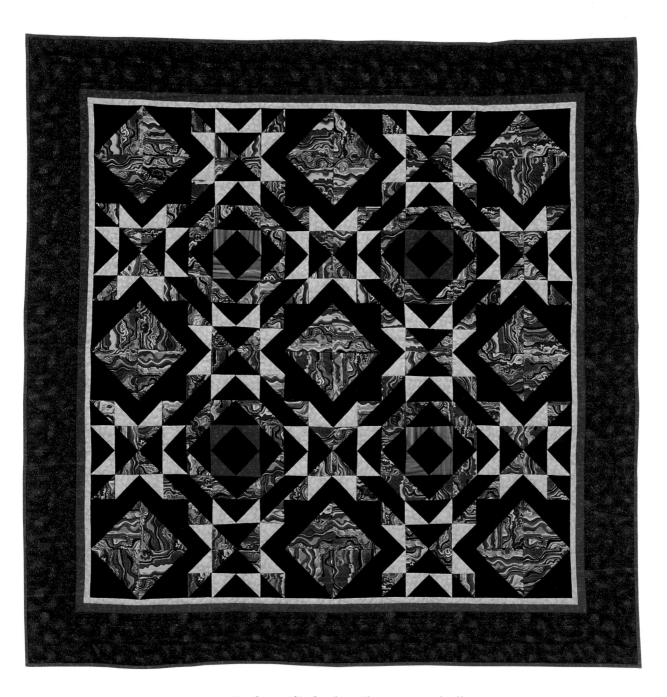

Tropical Twilight by Chris Campbell,
1995, San Jose, California, 51" x 51".

Using alternating blocks with a star variation, Chris created a quilt with a vibrant effect.

New England Paradise by Mona Woo,
1995, Cupertino, California, 39" x 39".

*Mona pulled fabrics from her French toile collection and combined
them with some of the current Smithsonian prints. The quilt is
reminiscent of autumn in New England. Machine quilted.*

The Stars Do Shine in Ramona by Carol O'Brien,
1995, Ramona, California, 61" x 61".

*Carol made this quilt in the midst of moving from
San Diego to Ramona. She called it her sanity project.*

Fractured Back by Karenina Grun-Louie,
1995, San Jose, California, 41½" x 41½".

*This quilt evolved on its own. The vibrant prints (many provided by
Hoffman of California Fabrics) set the pace. The name of the
quilt was inspired by the back art (see page 86).*

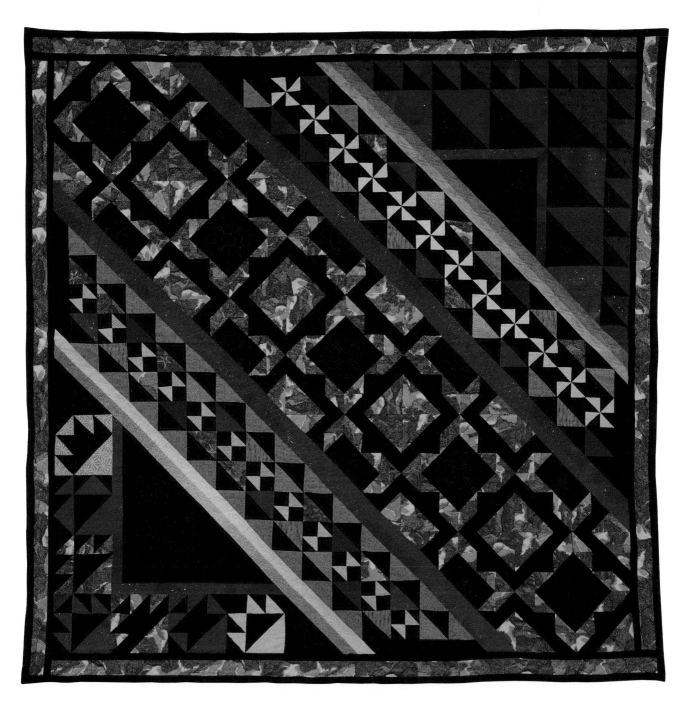

Rainbow's End by Anne DeRienzo,
1995, San Jose, California, 66" x 66".

*Anne combined a variety of block sizes and styles to
create this dazzling sampler quilt. Hand quilted.*

Nature's Glow by Carol A. Knight, 1995, Milpitas, California, 42" x 54".

While shopping for fabric, Carol was drawn to the Rising Sun Quilt Fabric Collection (RJR Fashion Fabrics), which is based on quilts in the Smithsonian's collection. From that moment, she knew she had to design a quilt representing the natural warmth and beauty of the sun. The quilt is embellished with Fimo beads and buttons. Hand quilted.

Tropical Dreaming by Lilly Thorne, 1995,
Abbotsford, British Columbia, Canada, 48" x 48".

*Tropical splendor, sunshine, and blue waters are things that relax Lilly
when she daydreams. The quilt is beautifully enhanced by machine
appliqué, embroidery, and beading. Machine quilted.*

Sedona by Constance Ann Boulay,
1995, Campbell, California, 50" x 50".

Connie's choice of fabrics and design was influenced by a recent trip to the Southwest. Soon after her trip, she attended a "Random Acts of Stripping" workshop. The quilt is the end result of both of these experiences. Hand and machine quilted.

First Born by Cooky Schock and Patty Barney,
1994, Campbell, California, 52" x 62".

This is where it all began. Using the Magic Base Block technique, we combined our scraps to make our first "Random Acts of Stripping" quilt. This is a true memory quilt. We spent the morning reminiscing about times past that each scrap evoked. Machine quilted by Sandy Klop.

Sunshine on Daffodils
by Ange Hampton-Mirer, 1995, San Jose, California, 31" x 39".

Ange hand dyed her own fabrics for this quilt, which was inspired by the daffodils that bloom in her garden every spring. The appliqué was designed by her sister, Jacqueline Hampton. Machine quilted.

Rosebud
by Sandy Andersen, 1995, El Cajon, California, 40" x 40".

Using hand-dyed fabrics, Sandy adapted the traditional Rosebud pattern to the Magic Base Block technique. She used the leftover small units to create her border.

There's Music in the Stars by Diana Cutting,
1995, Campbell, California, 39" x 48".

Diana's favorite theme of stars shines through with this quilt. It started with a fat-quarter packet and ended with a novelty fabric depicting dice that she purchased in Reno, Nevada. A touch of lamé gives it an overall sparkle. Machine quilted.

Off the Wall by Cooky Schock,
1995, San Jose, California, 45" x 45".

The color choices for this quilt were easy, the design layout was easy, but what to do with those big triangular areas?—so it stayed on the wall a long time. Finally, the inspiration came. Machine quilted by Sandy Klop.

Leaf Storm by Barb Haymond, 1995, San Jose, California, 55½" x 70".

Barb made this quilt for her husband to keep him warm during cool winter evenings while watching television. The inspiration for the block design and quilting pattern came from a bush maple tree. Hand quilted.

Connections by Selma Zinker, 1995, Santa Clara, California, 32½" x 52".

Selma wanted to create a feeling of movement and fluidity through the use of pinwheels and her choice of fabrics. She was highly motivated since she is about to become a first-time grandmother. She has since found out that twins are on the way. Hand quilted by Selma's daughter and soon-to-be aunt, Bobbie Zinker.

Magic Snowflake
by Shirley Ogisaka,
1995, Santa Clara,
California, 44" x 44".

Shirley wanted to make a quilt that was easy, yet visually appealing. The end result reminded Shirley of a paper-cut snowflake. Machine quilted.

Assembling and Finishing the Quilt

Blocks can be arranged in either a horizontal or diagonal setting and can look very different, depending on the setting. For additional variety, alternate blocks are added; these can be plain blocks or a second set of pieced blocks. Using alternate blocks reduces the number of pieced blocks you need to make. Alternate plain blocks also provide a perfect opportunity to show off your quilting skills. Combining traditionally pieced blocks with Magic Base Blocks opens up other design possibilities.

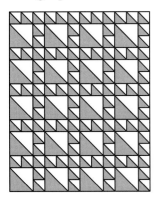

Horizontal or Straight Set

Diagonal Set

Diagonal Set with Plain
Alternate Blocks

HORIZONTAL SETTINGS

Horizontal settings (also called straight sets) are the easiest way to put a quilt together. Blocks are sewn together in vertical and horizontal rows. There are several methods that can be used. As with anything, there are advantages and disadvantages to each method. Here is what works best for us.

Patty likes chain piecing:

1. Starting at the bottom left-hand corner, pair the first 2 blocks from the last row (columns A and B), right sides together. Proceed up the first 2 columns, pairing the first 2 blocks from each row. Place these blocks to the left of your sewing machine, with the side to be sewn toward the machine.

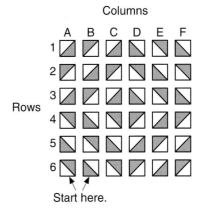

2. Chain-piece each pair of blocks. (See page 14.) Do not cut the threads between the pairs. When each column is completed, put it back on the design wall.

3. Proceed with pairs of blocks from the next 2 columns (C and D). Pair and sew them together as in steps 1 and 2. Continue in this manner until you have worked your way across the quilt. You should now have several columns of sewn blocks. This is a good time to double-check the placement of blocks in your design.

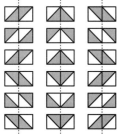

4. Sew the first 2 sets of columns together; proceed across the quilt. The horizontal rows are now completed and attached to each other by the unclipped threads.

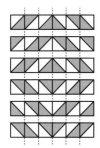

5. Press the seams in opposite directions from row to row. Sew the rows together, making sure to match the seams between the blocks.
6. Press the quilt top from the back side first, then from the front.

Cooky finds that constructing the quilt top in units works best for her. With this technique, you have only one long seam to match up.
1. Look at the block layout on your design wall. Visually divide the quilt top into 4 sections. (They may not always be equal sections.) Each section will be sewn separately.

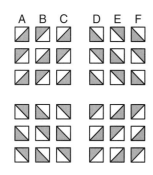

2. Chain-piece column A to B. Chain-piece column C to the AB set. Finger-press to create opposing seams.

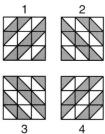

3. Sew the rows together horizontally. Complete each section before moving on to the next step.
4. Sew sections 1 and 2 together, then sew 3 and 4 together.

5. Sew sections 1/2 and 3/4 together.

DIAGONAL SETTINGS

Diagonal settings often scare a beginner, but this fear is unwarranted. With a little math (don't run away yet), the outside triangles will no longer be a problem.

If you are using alternate blocks, the first thing you need to know is what size to make them. They need to be the same size as your pieced blocks. Measure the pieced blocks to be sure. If your block is 7³/₄" (unfinished) and the quilt directions say it should be 8", cut the alternate blocks 7³/₄". Keeping your blocks a consistent size will help prevent your quilt from bowing in the middle.

Arrange all blocks on your design wall, then determine how many quarter-square triangles (side setting triangles) and half-square triangles (corner triangles) are required to finish the quilt.

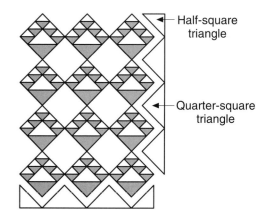

Half-square triangle

Quarter-square triangle

At first glance, you may wonder why you can't use half-square triangles around the outside of your quilt—it's easy to figure the size you need—but stop and think a minute. Do you want all those bias edges running around the outside of the quilt? There is a better way. Ready or not, here comes the math part.

Quarter-square triangles are used for side setting triangles so the straight of grain will be on the edge of the quilt. To determine the size you need, measure your finished block size (for our example, we'll use a 6" block). Multiply 6" by 1.414. (This is a magic number, and you really don't want to know where it came from, but trust us, it works.) Add 1¼" to the sum:

$$6" \times 1.414 + 1.25" = 9.73" \text{ or } 9\frac{3}{4}"$$

Cut a square this size, then cut the square twice diagonally to yield 4 quarter-square triangles.

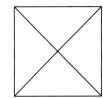

1 square yields
4 quarter-square triangles.

To determine how many squares to cut, divide the required number of side triangles by 4.

Half-square triangles are used for the corners so again the straight of grain will be on the edges of the quilt. To figure the size of the half-square triangles for the corners, divide the finished block size by 1.414 and add ⅞" (.875):

$$6" \div 1.414 + .875 = 5.12 \text{ or } 5\frac{1}{8}"$$

Cut a square this size, then cut the square once diagonally to yield 2 half-square triangles.

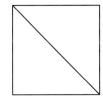

1 square yields
2 half-square triangles.

Place all the triangles in their appropriate positions on the design wall. From this point on, the construction of a quilt is similar to a straight set. The main difference is the blocks are sewn in diagonal rows instead of straight rows.

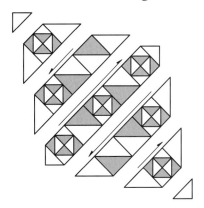

BORDERS

Borders add the finishing touch to a quilt, much like the frame around a picture. The borders should complement a quilt, not distract from it. There are no set rules in determining the width of a border, but here are a few guidelines that will help you keep things in proportion so the border does not overpower the quilt. Your quilt will usually tell you what kind of a border it wants. Many beginning quilters question the ability of a quilt to talk to its maker, but it does—trust us!

Little things mean a lot. Highlights (border accents) are ways to subtly add interest to a quilt. We feel that adding these narrow borders before the larger border gives the quilt extra pizzazz. By choosing one of the lesser-used colors, or even a color not used in the quilt, a highlight can help tie a quilt together.

Highlights often can turn a dull quilt into a dramatic one. In "If It Only Snowed in San Jose" (page 19), had we used just a large maroon border, it would have been OK, but by adding two narrow borders of gold and green, the quilt has a warmer feel. When you are adding highlights, be sure to audition lots of different colors. You might be surprised at the outcome.

Simple borders are often the perfect frame for a busy quilt pattern. They help focus the viewer's attention on the main body of the quilt. Certain fabric designs look best when the corners are mitered. Stripes, one-way designs, and border prints should always be mitered. The effect is worth the effort.

Sometimes your quilt calls for a more complex border. This is a chance to use up any extra parts left from the quilt body: small block units, extra strip sets, maybe even parts left over from another quilt. Refer to the "Block Dictionary" (pages 98–101) for some inspiring examples of borders that use leftover or planned pieces of Magic Base Blocks.

Whatever border you choose, it is important to cut the border strips the correct size before sewing them to the quilt. How often have you gone to a quilt show and noticed that some of the quilts do not hang straight? Did they wave at you? They shouldn't. In all probability, the quilter just cut and sewed the border strips on without first measuring and cutting them to the correct size. The waviness is caused by measuring improperly or not measuring at all. It might seem like you could simply cut long strips and sew them onto your quilt, but it just doesn't work that way.

The proper way to measure borders is to measure your quilt in three places, both horizontally (width) and vertically (length). Do not take these measurements at the outside edges of the quilt, which always seem to have a little flare, due to excess handling and pressing.

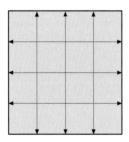

Add the three horizontal or vertical measurements, then divide by 3 to get the average width or length. It should not vary more than ½" from any of the original measurements. It is possible to gently ease up to a ½" difference without creating any distortion. A difference of more than ½" should be corrected before adding the borders.

Sometimes it is necessary to piece the border to get the required length. Place the seams a quarter to a third of the distance from a corner. This will be less noticeable than placing the seam at the center between two corners of the quilt.

Attaching Highlights and Straight-Cut Borders

The highlights and borders are measured, cut, and sewn in the same manner. You can attach the borders using the top-bottom, side-side sequence or the side-side, top-bottom sequence. It does not matter, as long as you are consistent with all the highlights and borders within each quilt.

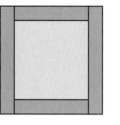
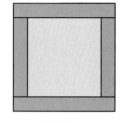

| Top-Bottom, Side-Side Sequence | Side-Side, Top-Bottom Sequence |

1. Using the average horizontal measurement, cut 2 border strips to that length, 1 for the top and 1 for the bottom.
2. Mark the centers of both the quilt top and the border strips with a pin.
3. Pin the borders to the top and bottom edges of the quilt, matching the center marks and ends. Ease as necessary. Sew the border strips in place using a ¼"-wide seam allowance. Press the seams toward the outer edges.

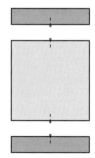

4. Repeat steps 1, 2, and 3 with the vertical measurements for the side borders.

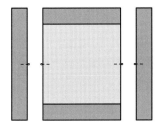

Note: We recommend backstitching at the beginning and end of the last border added. This particular seam takes a lot of stress before the quilt is finished.

Mitered Borders

Mitering borders takes a little time and thought, but the results are worth it. If using multiple borders and highlights, sew the strips together first and treat the resulting unit as one border. This makes mitering easier and quicker.

1. Estimate the finished outside dimension of your quilt, including borders (don't forget the highlights). Both of us add at least 4" total to this measurement for extra insurance. Nothing is more upsetting than to have a border that is 1" too short to miter the corners.
2. Mark the centers of both the quilt top and the border strips with a pin.
3. Pin a border strip to the quilt top, matching the center marks.
4. Stitch the border to the quilt top using a 1/4"-wide seam allowance. Begin sewing 1/4" from the corner of the quilt top, backstitch, and continue sewing the length of the seam. End 1/4" from the opposite corner with another backstitich. Press the seams toward the border. Add the remaining border strips in the same manner.

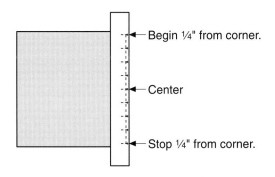

Begin 1/4" from corner.

Center

Stop 1/4" from corner.

5. Lay the quilt on a flat surface. Fold the quilt top diagonally and align the raw edges of the border strips.

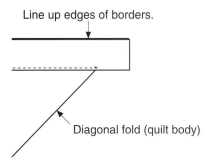

Line up edges of borders.

Diagonal fold (quilt body)

6. Align your ruler's 45°-angle line with the top edge of the border, and align the straight edge with the diagonal fold of the quilt. Be sure the inside corner where you backstitched is on the diagonal fold. Using a sharp pencil, carefully mark the diagonal line on the border. This will be the sewing line. Before you sew on the diagonal line, be sure to match and carefully pin any seams that must meet.

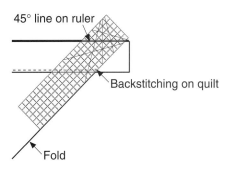

45° line on ruler

Backstitching on quilt

Fold

7. Sew from the outside edge to 1/4" from the inside corner; backstitich.

Note: Starting at the outside edge reduces the chances of having a flared corner. Backstitch at this outside edge for stability.

8. Trim the seam allowance to 1/4", but before making that crucial cut, open the quilt and make sure all points that should meet, do, and that the quilt lies flat. If things don't match up the way they should, you have the option of taking it apart and trying again because you haven't cut anything yet.
9. Press the seams open. Miter the remaining corners.

BACKINGS

Now that your quilt top is finished, it's time to consider the quilt backing. There are several options available, including a solid-colored backing, a multicolored print, or a pieced backing. Whichever you choose, it should relate in some way to the front of the quilt.

A solid-colored backing is a perfect way to show off your quilting skills. When picking a fabric for the backing, consider its relationship to the front. A light-colored quilt top should have a complementary backing. It would look strange to have a pastel front with a bright purple backing. A dark color could also shadow through to the front when it is quilted. The same holds true for a dark quilt top with a light backing, except that the effects would be reversed: the front would shadow through to the back of the quilt.

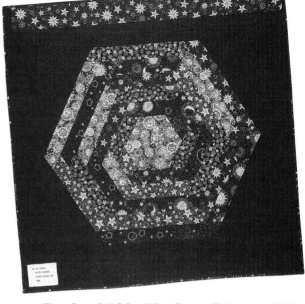

Back of "Oh, My Stars" (page 30)

There are advantages to using a multicolored print for the backing. It works well if you like to use different-colored threads in your quilting. It also camouflages less-than-perfect quilt stitches. Need we say more?

Pieced backings have taken on a whole new meaning, and they are now called "back art." They are a good way to use extra blocks, strips, or leftover fabrics. Pieced backings make a definite statement about a quilt and create an unexpected surprise when the quilt is turned over. There are several quilts in this book that feature back art; three are shown on this page.

Once you have decided on the type of backing you want, you have to figure out what size to make it. Measure the finished quilt top and add a minimum of 3" to each side. This is a good insurance policy. We both have had the experience of the layers shifting in the quilting process, which led to adding an extra strip to an already quilted backing. This is a lesson you only have to learn once!

**Back of
"Arctic Camouflage"
(page 20)**

**Back of
"Fractured Back"
(page 70)**

BATTINGS

There are many different types of battings, and it can get a little confusing when it comes time to choose one for your quilt. How your finished quilt will be used may determine the type of batting you choose. Will the quilt be laundered frequently, or will it be used as a wall hanging? Are you going to hand or machine quilt it, or are you going to tie it? Batting choices fall into three categories: natural fibers, man-made fibers, and blends.

Natural fibers include cotton, wool, and silk. Because they are natural, these battings breathe, keeping you warmer in winter and cooler in summer. They are easy to hand or machine quilt.

Man-made fibers include polyester. They come in a wide variety of densities, ranging from very thin to fat. One of the best advantages to using a man-made batting is its washability; it does not shrink. On the other hand, polyester does not breathe.

Blends combine the best qualities of both categories and are becoming very popular with quilters.

All prepackaged battings need to relax before use. Remove the batting from the packaging at least twenty-four hours prior to basting your quilt. Air is removed in the packaging process to condense the batting. By taking the batting out of the packaging and unfolding it, you are allowing it to breathe and regain its original size, shape, and fluffiness.

MARKING THE QUILTING DESIGN

Quilting is the icing on the cake. It enhances your piece by drawing attention to specific areas of the quilt. Quilting can be done either by hand or machine. There are several different types of quilting designs: outline, motif, grid line, meandering, and echo.

Outline quilting is done ¼" from the seam lines. This traditional type of quilting accents the piecing in the blocks.

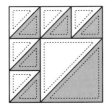

Motif quilting uses quilt stencils as a guide. Stencils come in a wide variety of designs and sizes. Some for continuous machine quilting are now available commercially.

Grid lines are used for background fill-ins and allover patterns. They can be parallel, diagonal, or straight lines, or they can be combined to create cross-hatching.

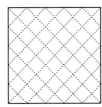
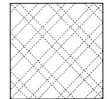

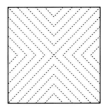

Meandering or stippling is an allover pattern created by random stitching. It is used very effectively as a background for motif quilting, setting it off.

Echo quilting, also known as Hawaiian quilting, outlines or echoes a repeated shape.

Some quilters prefer to mark their quilts prior to basting, especially if they have chosen a complicated design. It is not necessary to mark a quilt for machine quilting if most of the quilting will be done freehand or in-the-ditch. If you choose an original or complicated design, the quilt should be marked prior to basting. This applies to both hand and machine quilting.

There are numerous marking tools available to the quilter. Regardless of your choice, be sure you pretest the marker on a scrap of fabric. Does it wash out? Not every marker works with every fabric; always do a pretest.

That Patchwork Place publishes excellent reference sources on both hand and machine quilting: *Loving Stitches: A Guide to Fine Hand Quilting* by Jeana Kimball and *Machine Quilting Made Easy* by Maurine Noble. *Quilting Design Sourcebook* by Dorothy Osler includes thirty-five full-scale quilting motifs to use in your quilts.

BASTING

At this point, you now have a marked quilt top, batting, and a backing. The next step is to make a quilt sandwich and baste the layers together for quilting. Basting requires a large, flat surface. A floor with no carpeting (for those with good knees and backs) or a large tabletop works well.

1. Spread out the quilt backing, wrong side up. Pull it taut and tape or clamp down the edges of the backing. Remember, taut is not tight. If you release the tape or clamp, your fabric should not spring back. Be sure all four corners of the backing are square.

2. Smooth the batting over the backing, making sure there are no bumps or ripples. Do not stretch or pull the batting into place. There is no need to tape or clamp the batting.

3. Center the quilt top on the batting and backing, right side up. Smooth it out, making sure there are no wrinkles, bubbles, small pets, or children caught between the layers.

4. Safety pin the entire quilt sandwich at 6" intervals. This will keep the quilt from shifting while you are basting it. (If you are machine quilting, space your safety pins 4" apart and

eliminate steps 5 and 6. Avoid placing pins where you intend to machine quilt.)

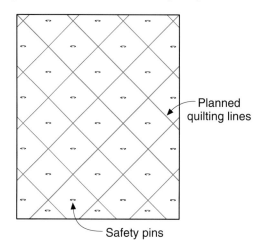

Planned quilting lines

Safety pins

5. Baste in a grid pattern, starting from the center of the quilt and working outward. Using a long needle and thread long enough to reach the outside edge, start stitching. Basting stitches can be anywhere from 1" to 2" long. Neatness does not count here. Space basting rows about 3" to 4" apart across the entire quilt surface.

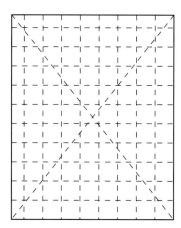

6. Complete the basting process by turning the excess backing and batting to the front of the quilt to cover the raw edges. Secure with a basting stitch all around the quilt. This protects the edges of the quilt from becoming frayed and worn during quilting. It also keeps little kitty claws away from the batting.

BINDINGS

Bindings are made using either straight-grain or bias strips. Both of us prefer bias binding. The edge of a quilt takes the most wear, and bias binding seems to be the sturdier of the two.

Making your own binding is easy. The fabric can be one of those used in the quilt body or a combination of fabrics. Plaids and stripes produce an interesting effect. Always prewash the fabric used to make the binding.

To determine how much binding you need, measure the perimeter of the quilt and add 10" to 12". The added inches allow for turning corners and joining the ends. It's always better to have too much than not enough.

We use bias strips cut 2" wide to make a French-fold (also known as double-fold) binding. Strips are cut using the tube method. Refer to "Yardage for Continuous Bias Binding" on page 93 to determine the amount of yardage needed to make the binding.

1. Cut a square of fabric the size given in the chart. Remove any selvage edges. Cut the square in half diagonally to form 2 triangles.

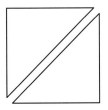

2. With right sides facing, sew the triangles together as shown, using a ¼"-wide seam allowance. The points of the triangles should overlap by ¼". When opened, the pieces will form a parallelogram. Carefully press the seam allowances open, keeping in mind that there are exposed bias edges.

 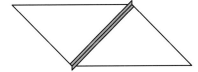

3. Use a sharp pencil and a long ruler to draw lines 2" apart, parallel to the longest sides. Trim any excess fabric after the last drawn line. Mark Xs on your fabric as shown.

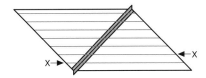

4. To form the tube, match the Xs and pin the edges, wrong sides together. The drawn lines should line up ¼" from the edges of the fabric. To check this, insert a pin on one drawn line ¼" in from the edge. It should come out on the corresponding pencil line on the opposite side. When you are through pinning, the finished shape will look strange; it should form a tube you can stick your arm through.

5. Sew the tube using a ¼"-wide seam allowance. Press the seam open.

6. Beginning at one end of the tube, cut along the pencil line until you have one long, continuous piece of bias.

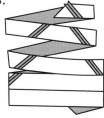

7. Press the length of the bias strip in half, wrong sides together. Remember, you are dealing with bias edges, so press (do not iron) to avoid stretching.

Attaching the Binding

1. Beginning about two-thirds from one corner of the quilt, place the binding and the quilt top right sides together, raw edges even. Begin sewing 3" from the end of the bias binding, using a ¼"-wide seam allowance.

Note: Use a walking or even-feed foot when attaching the bias binding. The layers are fed through the machine at an even rate, eliminating any shifting or puckering.

2. To miter a corner, stop sewing ¼" from the corner. Backstitch. Remove the quilt from the machine.

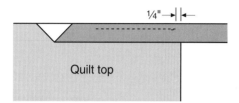

3. Fold the binding back onto itself, creating a 45° angle. Fold the binding back onto itself again, aligning it with the next edge. Begin sewing from the corner of the quilt. Backstitch and continue in this manner around the quilt.

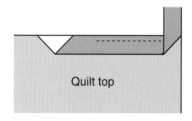

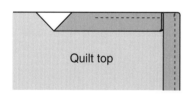

4. To connect the ends of the binding, stop sewing approximately 4" from the starting point. Cut the end of the binding so it overlaps the beginning by 1". Turn the ends under ¼" and finger-press. Tuck one end into the fold. Continue stitching, overlapping the beginning stitches; backstitch.

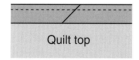

5. Turn the binding to the back of the quilt and hand stitch in place.

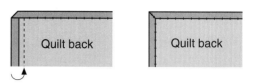

DOCUMENTING YOUR QUILT

There is one last step to complete your quilt. Make it easy on future generations by documenting your work on a quilt label. Labels can range from simple to elaborate but should include the following information: quilt title, quilter's name, date, city, and state. Feel free to add any pertinent information about the quilt. Was it made for a special occasion to honor someone, or was it your personal statement commemorating an event? Whatever label you use, make sure it is washable.

We hope you have enjoyed working with Magic Base Blocks as much as we have enjoyed presenting them to you. Every time we play on the design wall, we discover another possible arrangement we had not thought of before. We are sure you will also find this true. Have fun. This isn't The End, just the beginning.

DIAGRAMS FOR MAGIC BASE BLOCKS

Magic Base Block #1

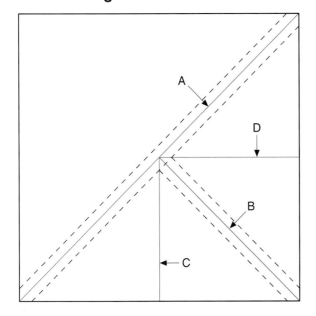

Legend: Cutting line ————————
Sewing line – – – – – – – –
(¼" from the diagonal cutting lines)

Preprinted grid papers for Magic Base Blocks are available. For more information, contact:
Patty Barney and Cooky Schock
P.O. Box 2068
Santa Clara, CA 95055-2068

Magic Base Block #2

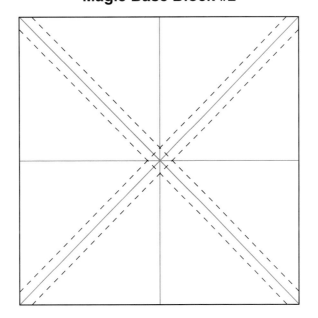

CALCULATING MAGIC BASE BLOCK SIZES

For use with both Magic Base Block #1 and Magic Base Block #2. When cutting Magic Base Block #2 for your pattern, cut it the same size as the Magic Base Block #1 you are using.

Four Patch Blocks

Formula: Divide the desired finished size of a Four Patch block by 4, multiply by 2, and add $1\frac{7}{8}$".

Finished Block Size	Cut Magic Base Block Size
4"	$3\frac{7}{8}$"
6"	$4\frac{7}{8}$"
8"	$5\frac{7}{8}$"
10"	$6\frac{7}{8}$"
12"	$7\frac{7}{8}$"

Five-Patch Blocks

Formula: Divide the desired finished size of a five-patch block by 5, multiply by 2, and add $1\frac{7}{8}$".

Finished Block Size	Cut Magic Base Block Size
5"	$3\frac{7}{8}$"
$7\frac{1}{2}$"	$4\frac{7}{8}$"
10"	$5\frac{7}{8}$"
$12\frac{1}{2}$"	$6\frac{7}{8}$"
15"	$7\frac{7}{8}$"

Seven-Patch Blocks

Formula: Divide the desired finished size of a seven-patch block by 7, multiply by 2, and add $1\frac{7}{8}$".

Finished Block Size	Cut Magic Base Block Size
7"	$3\frac{7}{8}$"
$10\frac{1}{2}$"	$4\frac{7}{8}$"
14"	$5\frac{7}{8}$"
$17\frac{1}{2}$"	$6\frac{7}{8}$"

Nine Patch Blocks

Formula: Divide the desired finished size of the Nine Patch block by 3, multiply by 2, and add $1\frac{7}{8}$". This will give you the necessary size to cut your Magic Base Block.

Finished Block Size	Cut Magic Base Block Size
3"	$3\frac{7}{8}$"
$4\frac{1}{2}$"	$4\frac{7}{8}$"
6"	$5\frac{7}{8}$"
$7\frac{1}{2}$"	$6\frac{7}{8}$"
9"	$7\frac{7}{8}$"
$10\frac{1}{2}$"	$8\frac{7}{8}$"
12"	$9\frac{7}{8}$"

Standard Bed Sizes

Size	Mattress	Comforter	Comforter with Pillow Tuck
Crib	27" x 52"	27" x 52"	—
Twin	39" x 75"	61" x 86"	61" x 104"
Full	54" x 75"	76" x 86"	76" x 104"
Queen	60" x 80"	82" x 91"	82" x 109"
King	76" x 80"	98" x 91"	98" x 109"

Yardage for Continuous Bias Binding

Cut 2"-wide bias strips for $\frac{3}{8}$" finished binding. Refer to page 89.

Length of Bias Binding	Fabric Required
64"	12" square
100"	15" square
144"	18" square
196"	21" square
256"	24" square
324"	26" square
400"	29" square
484"	32" square
576"	35" square

QUILTING SUGGESTIONS

Forest Primeval

Arctic Camouflage

Cotton Candy

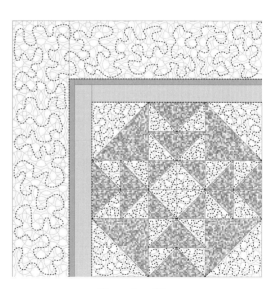

Canadian Star

Serengeti Eyes

What's Black and White and Red All Over?

Reflections

If I Had a Garden

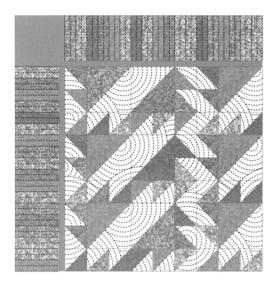

Spinning Hatchets

Broken Star

Oriental "Tee"

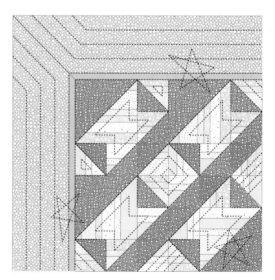

Oh, My Stars

Architectural Study

Stitch in Time

If It Only Snowed in San Jose

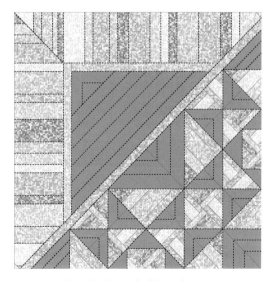

Jewels Come in Many Colors

BLOCK DICTIONARY

Four Patch Blocks

Five-Patch Blocks

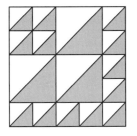 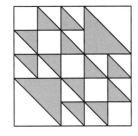 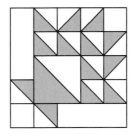 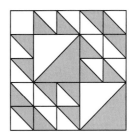

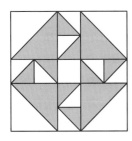 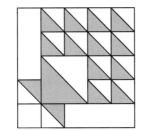 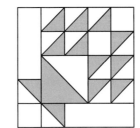 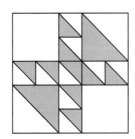

Seven-Patch Blocks

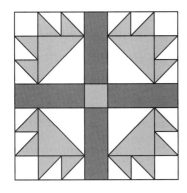 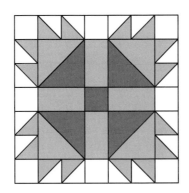 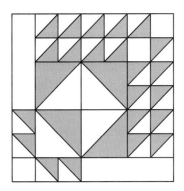

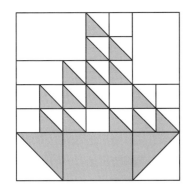 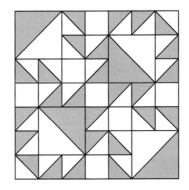 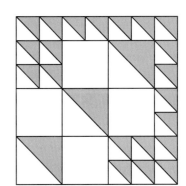

Nine Patch Blocks

Borders

Sample Settings

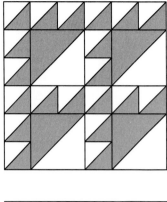
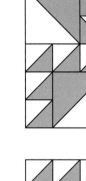
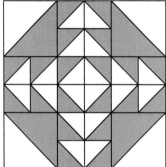
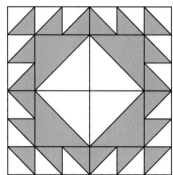
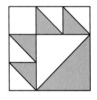
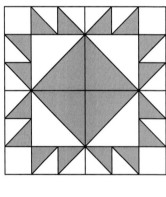
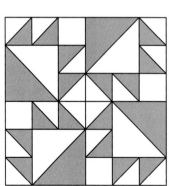
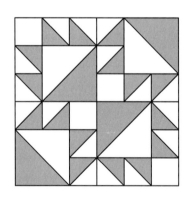
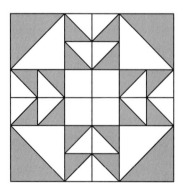

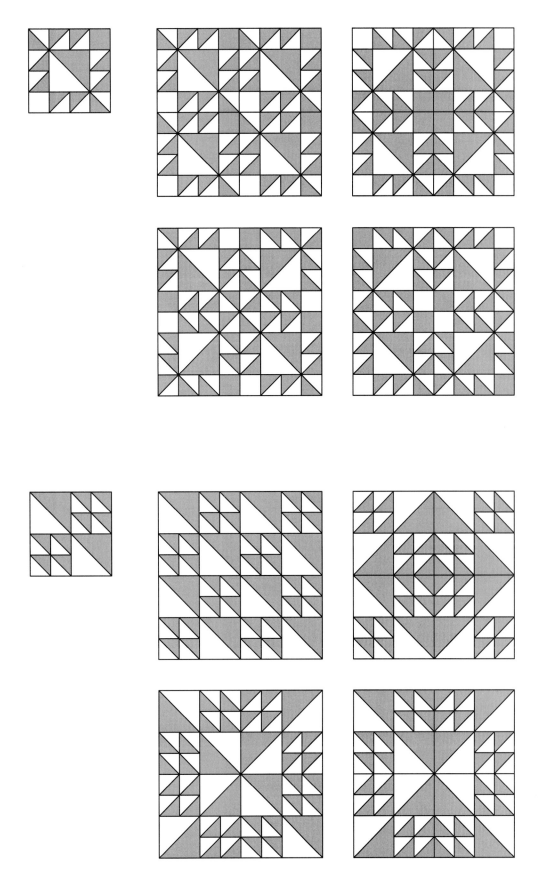

Publications and Products

4", 6", 8" & metric Bias Square® • BiRangle™
Ruby Beholder® • ScrapMaster • Rotary Rule™
Rotary Mate™ • Bias Stripper®
Shortcuts to America's Best-Loved Quilts (video)

Many titles are available at your local quilt shop.
For more information, write for a free color catalog
to That Patchwork Place, Inc., PO Box 118, Bothell,
WA 98041-0118 USA.

☎ U.S. and Canada, call **1-800-426-3126** for the
name and location of the quilt shop nearest you.
Int'l: 1-206-483-3313   Fax: 1-206-486-7596
E-mail: info@patchwork.com
Web: www.patchwork.com   8.96